Faith for
The Second Mile

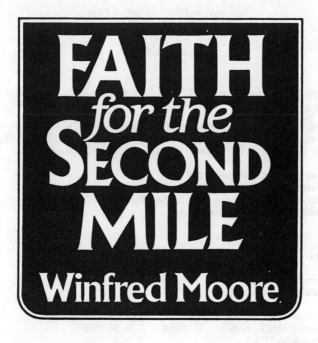

FAITH
for the
SECOND MILE

Winfred Moore

BROADMAN PRESS
Nashville, Tennessee

All Scripture quotations marked KJV are from the King James Version of the Holy Bible.

Unless otherwise indicated, all Scripture quotations are from *The New American Standard Bible* (NASB), © Copyright 1960, 1962, 1963, 1968, 1971, 1972, 1973, 1975, 1977 by The Lockman Foundation. Used by permission.

Dewey Decimal Classification: 248.4
Subject Heading: CHRISTIAN LIFE—SERMONS
Library of Congress Catalog Card Number: 86-9535
Printed in the United States of America

Library of Congress Cataloging-in-Publication Data

Moore, Winfred, 1920-
   Faith for the second mile.

   1. Christian life—Baptist authors.   I. Title
BV4501.2.M583   1986   248.4   86-9535
ISBN 0-8054-5726-7

To Elizabeth, my wife,
and to
our children,
Elizabeth Anne,
Fred,
and
Maria Elena

Contents

Contents

Faith for
The Second Mile

1

Faith for the Second Mile

You have heard that it was said, "AN EYE FOR AN EYE,
AND A TOOTH FOR A TOOTH." But I say to you, do not resist
him who is evil; but whoever slaps you on your right
cheek, turn to him the other also. And if anyone wants to
sue you, and take your shirt, let him have your coat also.
And whoever shall force you to go one mile, go with him
two. Give to him who asks of you, and do not turn away
from him who wants to borrow from you.

Matthew 5:38-42

No wonder the Jews, and even His own disciples, misunderstood the Lord Jesus Christ. His teachings then, as now,
run counter to the philosophies of the world.

The religious leaders of His day wanted to have Him
snuffed out, not only because they considered Him a blas-
phemer, but because of His teachings about the kingdom of
God and its nature.

Yes, Jesus was and is God, a perfect blending of God and
man, Immanuel—"God with us." He was hated then, as
many hate Him now, for His proclamation of the truth.

If the world hates you, you know that it hated Me before it
hated you. If you were of the world, the world would love
its own: but because you are not of the world, but I chose
you out of the world, therefore the world hates you. . . .
But they have done this in order that the word may be fulfilled that is written in their Law, THEY HATED ME WITH-
OUT A CAUSE (John 15:18-19,25).

By the laissez-faire standards of the world, the Sermon
on the Mount is a radical departure from business as usual.
Countless Christians have implored: "What? Does God expect me to live by those standards? That's unreal. Why,
those teachings are unattainable! This is a dog-eat-dog, cat-
scratch-cat world!"

Does God expect us to abide by the Sermon on the
Mount? Surely none of us would reject the validity of Jesus'
preaching. Yet, it would seem the overwhelming majority of
Christians live as though He never preached this heaven-
sent message.

From this passage of Scripture, Matthew 5:38-42, I key
in on one verse, 41: "And whoever shall force you to go one
mile, go with him two." What is even more amazing is the
word force (*compel* in the King James Version). Jesus is can-
didly teaching: Even if a person makes you perform a
slave's task, do more than the bare minimum. Exceed it. Go
beyond it.

Keep in mind that the Sermon on the Mount is a description of the blessings to be received, as well as the naming of
the type persons who are to be recipients of those blessings.
The Sermon on the Mount presents the techniques, if you

please, for living the Christian life, the "Christ-life"—not mere existence but superabundant life through Him. The Sermon graciously lays before us a working philosophy of life whereby we are acclimated to the times but anchored to The Rock.

When the Children of Israel were coming out of Egyptian bondage, en route to the Land of Promise, God gifted them with the Ten Commandments and a rather remarkable ecclesiastical and civil policy which was intended to govern all their interrelationships—with God, with one another, and with other peoples.

When the Lord Jesus came to establish His kingdom, a miraculous kingdom indeed, He emphasized that there must be a remarkable constitution and by-laws for the citizens of that kingdom. The Sermon on the Mount constitutes the constitution and by-laws for His subjects.

One of these by-laws is the precept of the second mile. When the Master laid down that law, it must have smitten His hearers. Consider their environment. They were living amid Roman domination and tyranny. The so-called "Pax Romana" had fallen over the land like a death pallor.

The populace was at the mercy of its foreign subjugators. Jesus had in mind a Roman law which demanded: If a Roman soldier came to your town—or even encountered you on the road—he could command you, "Pick up my baggage and packs. Carry them for me, Jew!" By explicit law you were required to carry that soldier's gear for *one mile*. That's all. One mile.

When you reached that distance (and they must have

counted in paces or either in prearranged increments) you could set the baggage down, sit on the ground, and in essence retort, "All right. You have your mile. I have carried your stuff. Now, you carry it the rest of the way. I've done my duty according to the law of Rome." And you might have mumbled under your breath, "You, rascal, you."

Jesus, realizing the paramaters of Roman law, delivered a different norm, "When you reach that milepost, if you are truly My child, you demonstrate that you belong to Me by voluntarily going a second mile—going twice as far as the law commands you to go."

Somehow I feel Jesus may have been thinking of that fateful day yet to come when Simon of Cyrene would be compelled to bear the cross that Jesus was physically unable to bear alone. Simon's service is recorded in all of the Synoptic Gospels.

Matt. 27:32—And as they were coming out, they found a certain Cyrenian named Simon, the man they pressed into service to bear His cross.

Mark 15:20-23—And they pressed into service a passerby coming from the country, Simon of Cyrene (the father of Alexander and Rufus), that he might bear His cross.

Luke 23:26—And when they led Him away, they laid hold of one Simon, a Cyrenian, coming in from the country, and placed on him the cross to carry behind Jesus.

At the same time I believe our Lord was looking down the centuries of time to the day when you and I live. His message for us is: Let My teachings so permeate and saturate your lives—and so crystallize into custom—that if you want to be considered a decent, respectable human being, you will be compelled and constrained to go one mile in every relationship of life.

But He does not stop there. By voluntarily doing more than the bare minimum, more than the legal requirement in all of our relationships, we demonstrate that we belong to Jesus.

All of us, regardless of our background or circumstances, are aware that the first mile is the common road. At this point I am reminded of the old Scottish folksong, "You take the high road, and I'll take the low road, and I'll be in Scotland before ye." High and low in the song have nothing to do with spiritual standards, and yet most of us, even Christians, take the spiritually low road.

We are accustomed to asking ourselves, *What's the comfortable, convenient way out?* Our churches are plagued with nominal Christians who are inconvenienced by going one mile, not to speak of two. The workplace is crammed with employees who would like to travel one-half mile rather than even one. Our entire world, in fact, is devastated by those on the spiritually low road.

So, it is not uncommon for most of us to do what we are compelled to do. Among us are many who yield to the compulsion of the first mile in their home relationships. For example, many a husband is faultlessly attentive to his wife in public—but never really considerate publicly or privately. Many a husband is polite but never affectionate.

Many a wife is publicly quite proud of her husband, but at

home she is hardly civil. In fact, she may express far more love for the dog or cat than her spouse! Maybe she's too polite to be mean, but also too selfish to express genuine kindness. Strangely enough, in spite of all the press about teen-age rebellion, some children obey every expressed command of their parents. Beyond that they do absolutely nothing thoughtful or kind toward their "old man" and "old woman."

And the question really is not, "Why are there so many divorces today?" The appropriate question is, "How do any of these families stay together?" Of course, more and more of them don't. Many of them stay together because of the law of respectability. Because moral and ethical values have eroded in our society, there are those who feel separation and divorce are respectable. "Why, everybody's doing it. Take old George. He left Marian, and he's just doing super. He's having a ball. And Susie's having the time of her life since she and Frank split!" As it appears to become "respectable" to break up, more and more will end up in the courts. I really do not want to sound "preachy," but what can you expect from a preacher? No wonder our nation is becoming a moral and spiritual basket case!

And there is also a first mile in our social life outside of the home. In my own city, many people I know wear a smile as they walk down the street—but that outward demeanor does not reveal what they genuinely are. They wear a smile fixed there by the expectations of the law of respectability. They observe customs and habits that do not express either their taste or their character, for they are no better in any way than self-interest and public opinion compel them to be. Some of those folks enjoy a reputation for beneficence that they no more deserve than I would if you put a six-shooter to my head and demanded my wallet—and I gave it out of compulsion and fear.

But there is also the same constraint in our business and professional life. In my state, and yours too, there are business persons boasting of the fact that they are honest and honorable. They brag about the idea that they always give one hundred cents on the dollar. They give thirty-six inches to the yard. They give sixteen ounces to the pound. And you'll look where shoulder blades used to be because you're sure they're sprouting cherub wings as you listen to them talk, as though the rest of us were not aware that there are penitentiaries and other unpleasant places for those who try to get by with ninety-nine cents to the dollar and thirty-five inches to the yard.

Then we view this in the employer-employee relationship. I have known of employers who have a fixed rule of never giving a salary increase to their employees unless they (the employers) are backed into a corner and compelled to do so. Each time the government has raised the compulsory minimum wage, some employers have all but died with apoplexy. Such Scrooges (pre ghosts) never make any concessions to the well-being of an employee and his/her family. *I mean, after all, with the economy being what it is, plenty of people are lined up waiting for your job!* That kind of one-mile employer thinks like that.

Before you employees say "Amen," there is another side

to the relationship. On the other hand, I have known employees who are not even one-mile workers, except when they are being watched. But "when the cat's away, the mice play." Some employees would take a week's pay for a day's work if they could swing it—and never have qualms of conscience.

If 5 o'clock is quitting time, and the boss is not around, when 5 comes, they are already at home with their shoes off sitting in front of the television set. No problem was ever solved between management and labor when they operated on a first-mile (or less) basis.

Amos had a choice word for unscrupulous employers and businessmen:

> Hear this, you who trample the needy, to do away with the humble of the land, saying,
> > "When will the new moon be over,
> > So that we may sell grain,
> > And the sabbath, that we may open
> > the wheat market,
> > To make the bushel smaller and the
> > shekel bigger,
> > And to cheat with dishonest scales,
> > So as to buy the helpless with money
> > And the needy for a pair of sandals,
> > And that we may sell the refuse of the
> > wheat?" (Amos 8:4-6).

Copious are the biblical admonitions concerning workers:

Prov. 6:6,9,10,11—Go to the ant, O sluggard [lazy person], Observe her ways and be wise. How long will you lie down, O sluggard? When will you arise from your sleep? "A little sleep, a little slumber. A little folding of the hands to rest," And your poverty will come in like an armed man.

Prov. 18:9—He also is slack [slow, negligent] in his work is brother to him who destroys.

Rom. 12:11—Not lagging behind in diligence, fervent in spirit, serving the Lord.

1 Thess. 4:11—And to make it your ambition to lead a quiet life and attend to your own business and work with your own hands, just as we have commanded you; so that you may behave properly toward outsiders and not be in any need.

2 Thess. 3:10,11—For even when we were with you, we used to give you this order: if anyone will not work, neither let him eat. For we hear that some among you are leading an undisciplined life, doing no work at all, but acting like busybodies.

Sad to note, but the first mile is also the measure of the Christian life and experience of far too many. What's wrong with the church? One-mile Christians. Many of us religiously do no more or go no farther than we are compelled to do or go. After all of these years of knowing Christ, many of us have not outgrown the initial question, "What must I do to be saved?" (Acts 16:31, KJV). Make no mistake—that is life's most strategic question until it has been asked and answered correctly.

But, beloved, could any of us be satisfied then, saved by the grace of God, redeemed from the bondage of sin, just to want that first step? Are we content to carry nothing but our own salvation into the presence of the Heavenly Father?

I refer here to those professing Christians who are always picking and choosing between Scriptures, trying to strike some kind of substandard bargain with God. Talk to them about the first mile, about tithing, about discipleship, and they invariably ask, "You don't have to do that to be saved, do you?"

Of course, you do not have to tithe to be saved. You do not have to travel that second mile to be redeemed. But you do have to go the second mile if you ever expect to "grow in grace, and in the knowledge of our Lord and Saviour Jesus Christ" (see 2 Peter 3:18, KJV). Yes, you have to do that to experience the "joy of the Lord."

> Hitherto have ye asked nothing in my name. Ask and ye shall receive, that your joy may be full (John 16:24, KJV).

Face it. You will never have "joy unspeakable and full of glory" (see 1 Peter 1:8, KJV) until you have acclimated to the second mile. There is no joy, no spiritual recompense in the first mile of any relationship. Will you, for a moment, travel with me along the course of the transcendent second mile?

Gentlemen, in the home the first mile is not the affection you feel for your wife. It is not that which you *have to do* in providing for the necessities of life on behalf of your wife and children. The second mile is bound up in those hundreds of little unrequested ministries. I speak about the expression of kindliness, love, and caring which will make her eyes sparkle and her face light up with heaven's glow. These "little things" will "through the years" make her joyful and thrilled all over again that she stood by you at the wedding altar and pledged her life, her love, her loyalty, her sacred honor to you . . ." 'til death do you part." That's the second mile.

For the wife it is not the well-ordered home she keeps, not the spick-and-span children who greet daddy at the end of a day's work. For a wife the second mile is that indescribable quality from her spirit like fragrance is inseparable from a gardenia or a rose. It is that inner sweetness which transforms any home into "home, sweet home." It causes a conscientious husband to declare, "There's no place like home!" That's the second mile. God help us to walk the second mile in our homes.

Frederick W. Robertson, the mighty British preacher of a bygone generation, wrote:

> Home is the one place in all this world where hearts are sure of each other. It is the place of confidence. It is the place where we tear off the mask of guarded and suspicious coldness which the world forces us to wear in self-defense, and where we pour out the unreserved communications of full and confiding hearts. It is the spot where expressions of tenderness gush out without any sensation of awkwardness and without any dread of ridicule.

God, give us second-mile homes!

In business, it is not merely being honest at work. It's not simply being there. It's the extra ounce to the pound, the extra inch to the yard, the extra cent to the dollar. One day after I preached this message, one of my hearers remarked,

"Whew, it's a good thing God called you into the ministry. You would've gone busted in business because that's not good business you're talking about."

Business people are always reporting about how keen competition is and how hard it is to make a profit. And the reason may well be: Most businesses are structured around the first mile. In the second mile, there are vacant lots for sale where one can build a business or a job, and there are gardens planted alongside each building site where the birds sing and where the flowers bloom indeed.

For the employer, the second mile is voluntarily granting a wage increase, because he can and because he wants to share the profits of business for the work. For the employee, it's the giving of himself for the sake of the enterprise as though the business itself belongs to him/her. It's putting *yourself,* not simply energy and time, into whatever the job may be.

Now comes the compelling question: "What is the second mile from a Christians standpoint?" The truly bona fide second mile is the Christian approach. That's the beauty of it, whether in the home or at work or in social life or in church fellowship. In every area I am to demonstrate that I am a child of God. Here is where the water hits the wheel, the place where my witness is felt, whether I go the second mile or pull up short.

In Matthew 5:47 (KJV), Jesus further enforces this inescapable truth:

> And if you greet your brothers only, what do you do more than others? Do not even the Gentiles do the same?

In other words, you as subjects of the kingdom are no better off than the *goiim*, the heathen, those outside the fold of God, *if* you do only what is expected and required. It's easy to greet a brother or a friend. It's easy to love those who love you. It's nothing special to accept a person of the same race, the same color of skin, the same background. Nothing to it.

Here Jesus' contrast was directed toward the publicans and also the religious leaders of the day.

Back up to verse 46:

> For if you love those who love you, what reward have you?
> Do not even the tax-gatherers do the same? (KJV).

The Lord looked at His followers, and His question must have stunned them. He was stressing, "The tax collectors, as bad and low-down as they are, love those who love them. They're kind to people who are kind to them. They'll do favors in return for those who do favors for them." But He was inquiring, "What do you, My followers, do that any non-Christians would not do?" Is there any difference in you? That is a profound question.

What do you and I do in the relationships of life that any unbeliever—although honest, hard-working, and moral— could not possibly do?

The best Christian has a besetting sin, a bugaboo. All of us have a chink in the armor somewhere, an embarrassing tendency, a proverbial skeleton in the closet. Sometimes the skeleton rattles out in the open air, unfortunately. Maybe all sins are *besetting*. My worst one is . . . a bad temper.

Thank God, it's not as bad as it used to be. The best-developed muscles in my anatomy are those which restrain my temper when I want to let it loose.

I will never forget when I was in Borger, Texas, and was trying to call the Baptist Building down in Dallas. I called in the day when you had to use an operator, and in a three-minute conversation, the connection was broken four times. Does that sound familiar?

The first time it was broken I was busy, and it irritated me. The second time it aggravated me. The third time, I was bonkers. The fourth time . . . well, I was completely beside myself. I had the receiver in one hand and the phone base in the other, bouncing it up and down on the desk to see if that would summon the operator.

I could hardly wait to hear that woman on the line so I could tell her what I thought of her and all the folks at the phone company. Yours truly never asked where the problem was—it didn't matter. I was inconvenienced and put out, and I wanted to bless somebody out. While trying to relocate the operator, it suddenly dawned on me: *Moore, there are three women in your congregation who are telephone operators.* You see how pious I am. *Man, if I bless one of those women out, she'll never tell me who she is, but next Sunday morning when I stand in the pulpit, wearing my black suit and with my Bible up close to my heart, she's going to be sitting right out there looking at me, saying, "Uh, huh, that sounds so nice this morning, but that's not the way ole Buster sounded last Thursday!"*

When the operator finally came on the line, I almost whispered in a sweet voice, "Please, Ma'am, somewhere down close to Dallas they've broken this connection again. Would you please see if you could reestablish my conversation?" Every time I saw one of those operators after that, I was thankful God takes care of some crazy preachers who don't have enough gumption to take care of themselves!

The fact is, I should have had enough of the spirit of Christ not even to think about losing control and reading the riot act to another person. When you control yourself, because the Spirit controls you, even in the most distressing circumstances, the second-mile principle is operative. I understand that even Al Capone and Bugsy Siegel could be nice when all was going to suit them. But what we as Christians need is second-mile living above all else.

So I preached this sermon at Borger. When I arrived home after the morning service, Hudson Davis, the owner of Davis Chevrolet, was standing by my front door. When you're a pastor, that's nearly always a bad sign. It makes you nervous, causes your hands to sweat, and conjures up all kinds of terrors.

Hudson was quick about his business. "Preacher, I want you to come over and preach this sermon at my place of business. We're going to have a second-mile campaign at Davis Chevrolet. I want to see if all of this you've been preaching really works." I did. They were going to invite me back three months later and have a report from all of their employees about the effectiveness of the second-mile campaign. Incidentally, it went well.

Right after I preached to Davis's employees, I bought four new tires from them to be mounted on my car. They were tubeless, but I was never a devotee of tubeless tires—felt they were unsafe. So, I had them put tubes into my tubeless tires.

So, I was driving down to Dallas and then to Sanderson (Texas) to ordain Gene Mederis who became one of our foreign missionaries. Driving out of Fort Worth—it was awfully hot and I had no air conditioning—I felt the right rear of the car going bumpety-bump. I climbed out. Sure enough, the tire was flat. Brand-new tire! I soiled my preacher hands changing the tire. I was wringing wet with sweat.

I crawled back in and hadn't gone a mile until I felt that ominous bump on the left side. To make a long story short, I wound up with four flat tires! A fellow at a service station broke one of the tires down and found the trouble. The fellow back at Davis's had installed valve cores that go with tubeless tires. Since I had tubes put in, the tubeless cores were not necessary.

There I was with four ruined tires. I could hardly wait to call Hudson Davis. I wanted Hudson, not an associate. I wanted to bless him out for the stupidity of his employees. While I waited for a slow service station man to make change, yep, it dawned on me that I was preaching to Davis's folks only a week before—on going the second mile.

I had boots put in the tires, limped on home, and the following day reported to Davis about the tires. We all had a good belly laugh. Once again the Lord took care of me. I didn't bless out anybody. I hate to admit it. It wasn't because

I had second-mile faith. It was because the Lord does build His hedge around us.

But guess what happened. I had the honor of baptizing thirty-five people from Davis's organization. Many of them testified, "If a man who knows Christ can take a deal like this in the spirit you took it, I want to know Him, too."

That was around thirty years ago. I still pass through there now and then. Only a few of those employees are still there, but the ones who are don't greet me with, "Hello there, how are you?" They always laughingly ask, "How are your tires?" Thirty years later!

Most of us in Christian work, I am afraid, are too often like the poet:

> Whatever I said in anger,
>   Whatever I said in spite;
> I'm sorry I spoke so quickly,
>   I thought up some worse ones last night!

How are you walking? Are you still living out of compulsion or oughtness? Is your faith as a Christian less than a mustard seed? Is it still business as usual? Are you missing the inexpressible joy, the exhilaration of the second mile?

Jesus is calling you to walk the second mile with Him.

> Lord, help me to live from day to day
> In such a self-forgetful way
> That even when I kneel to pray
> My prayer shall be for—Others.
> . . . .
> And when my work on earth is done,

And my new work in heaven's begun,
May I forget the crown I've won,
While thinking still of—Others.
· ·
Others, Lord, yes, others,
Let this my motto be,
Help me to live for others,
That I might live like Thee.

        —C. D. Meigs

2

Good News

For I am not ashamed of the gospel, for it is the power of God for salvation to everyone who believes, to the Jew first and also to the Greek.

Romans 1:16

But even though we, or an angel from heaven, should preach to you a gospel contrary to that which we have preached to you, let him be accursed. As we have said before, so I say again now, if any man is preaching to you a gospel contrary to that which you received, let him be accursed.

Galatians 1:8-9

From time immemorial we seem to have heard the expression, "It's the Gospel truth!" Yet, what you sometimes hear from folks may be factual or a reality but not "Gospel truth."

There is nothing in the Gospel that is not "good news." This is easily and quickly seen in Paul's description of the Gospel in 1 Corinthians 15:1-4:

Now I make known to you, brethren, the gospel which I preached to you, which also you received, in which also you stand, by which also you are saved, if you hold fast the word which I preached to you, unless you believed in vain. For I delivered to you as of first importance what I also received, that Christ died for our sins according to the Scriptures, and that He was buried, and that He was raised on the third day according to the Scriptures (1 Cor. 15:1-4)

There are many truths in the Word of God which are not related directly to the Gospel. It is a truth of God's Word that all are sinners. Yet, there is no good news in that pronouncement. "All have sinned and come short of the glory of God" is a statement of bad news and condemnation. All who have not repented will be punished for their sin of unbelief and refusal to accept the Gospel.

Years ago a boy played hooky from school. He left home as he always did, his books in a leather strap slung across his shoulder. He headed down the country lane toward the one-room school.

On that particular day he made another turn and went to the old river run where he fished all day. As the sun reached about the same place in the heavens as he would be returning from school, he put away the trot line, picked up his books, and trudged toward home.

As he came close to the yardgate, he began whistling to keep up his courage. As he stepped to the porch and reached for the handle of the ancient screen door, he became aware of unusual circumstances. The form of his father was on the other side of the door.

You see, his father was not ordinarily at the house when the boy came home from school. But the lad was not left to wonder for long, for the voice of the father came through that screen door, "Winfred, I must punish you for playing hooky." What my father said was the truth, but I can assure you it was not good news! It was far less than good news when he straightway carried out his promise in the wood-shed.

It is a truth from God's Word that man in his sin cannot deliver himself. That is not good news to human beings. It is not good news for a person to know he is a sinner, that his sins must be suffered for, and that he cannot save himself.

A fair-haired, blue-eyed little girl was very sick. The young mother had done all she could possibly do. Her only medicines were aspirin and cold cloths for the girl's feverish brow. Finally, the mother asked the father to go for the doctor. He sped the seventeen miles to summon the doctor.

When he arrived the old country doctor sat down in the cane-bottom chair. He made due examination while the young parents stood behind him, holding each other for comfort and courage. Finally, the old doctor gave the report, "I hate to tell you, but your child has polio."

The young mother almost screamed, "Oh, doctor, don't tell me my baby has polio, for there is nothing I can do to help her!" The diagnosis was correct, but it was certainly not good news. But then the doctor followed up with a ray of good news, "I believe we've caught it in time. If you do what I tell you to do, we might be able to bring her through without any crippling effect." That prognosis was also accurate, and that is where the good news came!

What, then, is the Gospel?

It is the declaration, the revelation that God loves us "with an everlasting love" (see Jer. 31:3), that He loves us to the extent that He sent His only begotten Son to make the Good News possible through the Cross. The first verse nearly every child learns is: "For God so loved the world that he gave his only begotten Son, that whosoever believeth in him should not perish but have everlasting life" (John 3:16, KJV).

To most of us that is not even "news" since we have heard it since our childhood days. It is sad that many of us have lost the thrill of that good news announced by the angelic messenger, "I bring you good tidings of great joy, which shall be to all people, for unto you is born this day in the city of David, a Saviour which is Christ the Lord" (Luke 2:10-11, KJV).

It was good, glorious news when those angels proclaimed it and when our own Lord and Savior embodied it and when Paul enthusiastically "declared unto you the gospel" (see 1 Cor. 15:1, KJV). In places where the Gospel has never before gone, it is the greatest news ever heard.

> We have a gospel to proclaim,
> Good news for men in all the earth;
> The gospel of a Savior's name:
> We sing His glory, tell His worth.
>
> Tell of His death at Calvary,
> Hated by those He came to save,
> In lonely suff'ring on the cross;
> For all He loved His life He gave.

. . . .
Now we rejoice to name Him King:
Jesus is Lord of all the earth
This gospel message we proclaim:
We sing His glory, tell His worth.
                              —Edward J. Burns

First John 4:10 says, "God is love." Not simply that He loves, but that He is love. The Gospel declares that the very essence of God's nature is love. In 1 Corinthians 13 Paul tells us what love is. In that chapter, if we substitute God for the word love, we will have a better grasp of the meaning of the Gospel.

One of our missionaries tells of another missionary to India, going to a Hindu village to preach his first sermon to a group of low-caste women who sat half-naked with their little naked babies in their laps. He chose as his text "God is love," and then began his message.

Soon one of the women timidly raised her hand and inquired, "Sir, what is love?" The missionary, perplexed, thought, *How shall I ever preach to these people about my God, whose very nature is love, when they do not know the meaning of love?* He turned to the woman and asked, "How do you feel toward the baby on your lap?" She replied, "Sir, how do I know how I feel toward my baby? I am a low-caste and ignorant woman. I just have a kind of going out of my heart toward my child." "That's it," replied the missionary. "God has a going out of His heart toward you."

Isn't it good news to know God has a going out of His heart to us? When we have sinned, when we have fallen short, when we have stumbled, when we have disappointed our Lord, isn't it wonderful to realize He loves us?

Yes, the first step toward embracing the Gospel is to recognize we are lost without Jesus Christ. "All we like sheep have gone astray: we have turned every one to his own way, and the Lord hath laid on him [Jesus] the iniquity of us all" (Isa. 53:6, KJV). "All have sinned and come short of the glory of God" (Rom. 3:23, KJV). "For the wages of sin is death, but the gift of God is eternal life through Jesus Christ our Lord" (Rom. 6:23, KJV).

Part of the message in God's Word is bad news—no doubt about it—for those who have never received Jesus Christ. They have nothing to look forward to but a Christless grave and an eternity in hell separated from God and all that is good and lovely and truly desirable. When the preacher of the Lord Jesus proclaims the message faithfully, he is saying in essence, "I have good news and bad."

But did you notice the second half of Romans 6:23, "But the gift of God is eternal life through Jesus Christ our Lord"? What a thrilling message of good news we have! "We've a story to tell to the nations."

God is love and when we come to Him through the Lord Jesus, He puts away our sins from us. I love that old alliterative phrase—He puts away the payment, penalty, and punishment of our sins. Hallelujah! All of the handwriting against us is blotted out. He remits our sins, redeems us from our sins, and reconciles us to God. "He will again have compassion on us: He will tread our iniquities under foot. Yes, Thou wilt cast all their sins into the depths of the sea" (Mic. 7:19).

> As far as the east is from the west So far has He removed our transgressions from us (Ps. 103:12).

> AND THEIR SINS AND THEIR LAWLESS DEEDS I WILL RE-MEMBER NO MORE (Heb. 10:17).

What does He do with our sins when we repent and turn by faith to the Lord Jesus Christ? He remembers our sins no more. He has an amazing power of forgetfulness when He wants to forget! He removes our sins from us—and from Him. "For Thou hast cast all my sins behind Thy back" (Isa. 38:17c). Hear that? Cast all of our sins behind His back! I remember that old song, "Praise God, My Sins Are Gone." One verse went, "They're underneath the blood on the Cross of Calvary, as far removed as darkness is from dawn."

> I once lived in a small town where the primary form of entertainment was to sit outside the Post Office, chatting, whittling, and listening to the talk that went on. One day a group of men sat on the porch steps, discussing all the things God could do. Finally an old black man said, "There's one thing God can't do." The others looked up, shocked. "God can't see my sins after they've been covered with the blood."[1]

Many of us defeated Christians go fishing for our sins. We try to remove them from the bag where God has buried them, and we count them over and over again, crying: "Oh, dear God, how I wish I'd never committed this sin or that sin." It is a sin to dig up what God has buried, to remember what God has forgiven and forgotten.

Let that sink in. Every sin of yours and mine that God has forgiven is buried, is drowned, is cast away, is removed—and can never be recalled, because somehow in His amazing grace, God has forgotten all about them. The omniscient, all-wise, all-knowing God has deliberately decided to forget our sins when we have confessed them and turned them over to Him.

A child was sent to the chalkboard by the teacher. There he was to work a problem in arithmetic. The more he worked, the farther from the answer he came. "Johnny, you don't have the right answer," the teacher critiqued him.

"Yes, Ma'am, I know that," Johnny answered.

"Johnny, I don't believe you can work the problem."

"No Ma'am, I can't," mumbled Johnny. "Help me."

The teacher came forward, holding the book, and explained, "Look, Johnny, you have subtracted where you should have added; you divided where you should have multiplied." Then she showed him how to do the problem. Then the two of them checked the answer in the back of the book. It was exactly the same as the one on the board.

Then with the eraser, the teacher wiped the board clean, handed Johnny the book and the chalk, and suggested, "Now, Johnny, you work it."

That is the Gospel. Christ does not dwell on telling me I have it wrong or I cannot get it right. I already know that within my heart and through the conviction of the Holy

Spirit. He comes to help me with the problem and then to wipe it clean. Then He gives it back to me, asking me to live for Him—more importantly for Him to live in me.

There are detractors from this message who chide, "That's too simple, too easy." They claim that salvation and forgiveness cannot be that plain and unvarnished. They want to mix in good works and human merit. Remember that forgiveness, in essence, is always the same.

How did Jesus forgive Simon Peter? He had warned Peter, "You will deny me three times before the rooster crows in the early morning." Peter had argued with Jesus, "Lord, you don't have to worry about me. I'll never do that. I'll never forsake you. The rest of these disciples may turn-coat on you, but not me!"

Then Peter did exactly the opposite. He denied his true identity and denied his Lord, as Jesus had prophesied.

After Jesus was raised from the dead, He appeared along the shores of Galilee. In today's language Jesus would have asked, "Fellows, do you have anything to eat? Let the nets down on the other side of the boat." John remembered the Lord's voice and yelled out, "It's the Lord." I think he yelled. I don't think he was able to be "laidback."

Peter could hardly wait for the boat to reach the shore. He jumped in and swam to shore. Same impetuous guy—but with a difference.

If Jesus would have been like some of us (thank God He is not!), He would have been shaking His finger in Peter's face before the water was out of his eyes, scolding him with, "I told you what you would do, you traitor, and you did it pre-

cisely as I said you would." But there was not one word of
rebuke from the Master when Peter reached shore.

First they had breakfast. Then Jesus called Peter aside.
The Lord could have embarrassed Peter in the presence of
the others but did not. If you have been a Christian any
length of time, you can probably recite this encounter almost from heart. Gently, I am sure, Jesus asked Peter,
"Simon, do you love Me?" He posed that question three
times, the same number of times Peter had denied his Lord
on that fateful night and that early morning when Jesus was
being scourged and tried. Three times the question and three
times the answer, "Yes, Lord, you know I love You."

Except for a leper Jesus sent to a priest for a clean bill of
health (Jesus had already cleansed and healed him), the
Master never sent a sinner away to make a sacrifice or to
visit a priest. It was always, as to the woman caught in the
very act of adultery, "Go and sin no more" (John 8:11*b*).
Jesus is in the business of redeeming and saving sinners.

> There is never a guilty sinner,
> There is never a wandering one,
> But that God can in mercy pardon
> Thro' Jesus Christ, His Son.

> Wonderful, wonderful Jesus,
> In the heart He implanteth a song:
> A song of deliverance, of courage, of
>   strength,
> In the heart He implanteth a song.
> —Annie B. Russell

Every Lord's Day people attend our churches with mis-spent lives, partly wasted in misdeeds and selfishness. What can be done? They must proceed to Calvary. There they must hand over those stained, soiled, sinful lives—and let the Lord cleanse them and return it to them clean and fresh.

No doubt you older readers have heard the story—and it is only a story—of the poor woman who lived in a European kingdom. Her daily existence was miserable and wretched, but she heard the king was coming through her hamlet.

She "gussied up" as best she could. At least her tattered and patched clothes were clean, and she donned her best bonnet, although it was frayed. She reminds us of the widow and her two mites. She had a copper coin which was almost worthless.

The poverty-stricken woman heard the king's procession was going to pass through the streets near her hovel. Rushing out into the cobblestone street, she heard the trumpets sounding, the cheers of the crowd, and the approaching hoofbeats and noise of the king's royal carriage.

She could hardly believe her eyes as the king's coach stopped in front of her lowly abode. The king himself climbed out of the carriage, and the woman, beside herself, curtsied and, in embarrassment, blurted out, "Your Highness, this is all I have, but I want you, my king, to have it," placing her pitiful coin into his ring-bedecked hand.

"Thank you, dear lady," he answered, "but I want you to have it back." Blushing and hurt, the poor woman accepted the coin. The king bade her adieu, returned to his carriage, and away it sped. With downcast eyes she opened her hand. Instead of a copper coin, there was a magnificent gold piece. The copper had turned to gold upon the touch of the king's hand!

And that's how it is with our pathetic lives, seemingly cheap, insignificant, meaningless. When we place them into the hands of the King, they are given back to us as priceless vessels for service in His Kingdom. As the old man expressed it, "I'm not much, but I'm all I got." Maybe we're not much in our eyes, but we are precious in the sight of Jesus. Why do you think He came to die for us, to give His life a ransom for our sins? "Red and yellow, black and white, they are precious in His sight. Jesus loves the little children of the world." And He loves us big children, too.

But you ask, "What about the justice of God? Isn't it going to be satisfied?" He is sinless and holy. We are sinful and unholy. He is righteous, and we are unrighteous. Yes, I declare that justice must and will be satisfied, but how is it to be satisfied? Is it pleased by revenge?

Two friends have a falling out. One testifies of the other, "He has done me wrong. I will get my revenge." So he shoots his former friend, and the friend is dead. Is the offended murderer satisfied? As long as he lives, the blood of his friend will haunt his conscience.

A father has a son who steals or who deals in dope. He exhausts every avenue of trying to help his son straighten out. In exasperation, the father finally instructs the police,

"Lock the boy up." Is the father satisfied? His heart is in the jail cell with his wayward boy.

It is not punishment or revenge which really satisfies. It is curing the loved one of what is terribly wrong with him.

And He said to him, "YOU SHALL LOVE THE LORD YOUR GOD WITH ALL YOUR HEART, AND WITH ALL YOUR SOUL, AND WITH ALL YOUR MIND." This is the first and foremost commandment (Matt. 22:37-38).

We should love God with all of our being—all our heart, all our soul, all our mind. We do not as sinners, but God has set out to win our love. We care more for money, pleasure, and human acclaim than we do for God. And Jesus wants to cure us, to heal us, to deliver us, to rescue us, to save us. Jesus "paid it all," the hymn goes. He has done that for us when we could not do it for ourselves. Mankind so desperately wants to save itself but cannot.

Salvation is ours for the asking. As in Luke 14, Jesus bids us today, "Come, all things are ready." The feast is prepared. The table is set. The invitation is extended.

A farmer, with three little children, buried his wife, their mother. After several months he announced that he was going into town to have a wedding ceremony. He would soon be home with a new wife for himself and a new mother for them.

Seeing their disappointment, he explained, "Children, I cannot work the fields and make a living for you and look after you at the same time. I need a wife. You need a mother. I am going to town to be married. We will be home in a few hours. You be sure to be neat and have clean clothes on when we return."

In a few hours the farmer was back with his new bride. They opened the door to view the three little ones, two tow-headed boys, a fair-haired little girl, all backed into a far corner. Looking up from under furrowed brows, this new mother, being especially wise in the ways of children, thought in her own mind, *Ah, little ones, I know what you're thinking. I know what you're saying. You're saying, "You're not our mommy. We won't have you for our mommy. We don't love you, and we will not love you!"* But she said in her heart, *Little ones, I'll find a way to help you love me.* And she did. She found a way so that those children, even when they were grown, never allowed anyone to refer to her as their "stepmother." She found a way. She loved them until they loved her in return.

And God, through His good news, speaks. "I will find a way into your hearts. I want you to love Me. I want you to be like Me. I want to have fellowship with you. I will find a way!"

That is the Gospel, the good news of God's love for us. A. C. Archibald, grand Canadian preacher of a former generation, wrote:

> No one can fathom it, but as we stand beneath the Cross of Christ, we realize that here is God's great transfusion for a dying world. To refuse what God offers in that Cross is to perish. To accept it is to live. This is the breadth and the length of the love of God that passeth knowledge. [2]

3

Don't Miss the Point

Then said Jesus unto them again, Verily, verily, I say unto you, I am the door of the sheep. All that came before me are thieves and robbers: but the sheep did not hear them. I am the door: by me if any man enter in, he shall be saved, and shall go in and out, and find pasture. The thief cometh not, but for to steal, and to kill, and to destroy: I am come that they might have life, and that they might have it more abundantly.

John 10:7-10, KJV

Jesus had a clear-cut purpose for coming into this sin-benighted world. In John 10 is one of His summary statements: "The thief cometh not, but for to steal, and to kill, and to destroy: I am come that they might have life, and that they might have it more abundantly" (v.10, KJV). Jesus knew precisely why He was here and what He had to do in order to fulfill His mission.

In Matthew 16 the Lord asked His disciples: "Whom do men say that I the Son of man am?" There was discussion about what others thought, but then Jesus implored:

"Whom say ye that I am?" Good ole Peter, in spite of his shortcomings, nearly always had a ready answer. He came back with, "Thou art the Christ, the Son of the living God." And Jesus commended him for that pivotal confession: "Blessed [exceedingly happy] art thou, Simon Bar-jona: for flesh and blood hath not revealed it unto thee, but my Father which is in heaven" (see vv. 13-17, KJV). Jesus was and is the promised Messiah. He didn't miss the point.

In the following chapter the Lord Jesus prophesied His atoning death: "The Son of man shall be betrayed into the hands of men: And they shall kill him, and the third day he shall be raised again" (17:22-23, KJV). He didn't miss the point.

Then, in Matthew 20, He taught His followers the lesson of ministry:

> But whosoever will be great among you, let him be your minister; And whosoever will be chief among you, let him be your servant: Even as the Son of man came not to be ministered unto, but to minister, and to give his life a ransom for many (vv. 26*b*-28, KJV).

The Messiah . . . but also a minister to others. He didn't miss the point.

In Mark's Gospel, the high priest inquired of Jesus: "Art thou the Christ, the Son of the blessed?" Without hesitation the Lord affirmed His Messiahship: "I am: and ye shall see the Son of man sitting on the right hand of power, and coming in the clouds of heaven" (see Mark 10:60-62, KJV). Jesus didn't miss the mark.

And He didn't miss the point when He revealed His divine mission at the synagogue in Nazareth. Reading from Isaiah 42, He then returned the scroll to the "minister" (rabbi or perhaps a layperson). "And he began to say to them, This day is this scripture fulfilled in your ears" (Luke 4:21; see also 2:16-18,20*ff.*, KJV). The Scripture He had read was a prophecy of the Messiah, the Redeemer, the Savior, the Deliverer of Israel.

> The Spirit of the Lord is upon me, because he hath anointed me to preach the gospel to the poor; he hath sent me to heal the brokenhearted, to preach deliverance to the captives, and recovering of sight to the blind, to set at liberty them that are bruised, To preach the acceptable year of the Lord (4:18-19, KJV).

Jesus didn't miss the point. And the congregation didn't either.

Jesus didn't miss the point of His Saviorhood. "I came not to call the righteous, but sinners to repentance" (Luke 5:32, KJV). "For the Son of man is not come to destroy men's lives, but to save them" (Luke 9:56, KJV). "For the Son of man is come to seek and to save that which was lost" (Luke 19:10, KJV).

Jesus came right to the point in the Gospel of John. He referred to Himself as the Water of eternal life (chapter 4), the Living Bread (chapter 6), the Light of the world (chapter 8). In chapter 10 He called Himself "the door of the sheep" (v. 7) and "the good shepherd" (v. 11). And there is our text, smack in the middle of John.

Why all my emphasis on Jesus' view of Himself and His ministry?—because I want you to see that He didn't miss the point. And He does not want us, His followers, to miss the point!

Perhaps you are one of those who was forced to read *Silas Marner* while in junior high or high school. Count yourself blessed if you caught the point of it—a wasted life. The author, George Eliot, wrote of Marner: "His life had reduced itself to the mere functions of weaving and hoarding, without a contemplation of an end towards which the functions tended. . . . So year after year Silas Marner had lived in this solitude, his guineas rising in the iron pot, and his life narrowing and hardening itself more and more into a mere pulsation of desire and satisfaction which had no relation to any other being."

All around us are those who have missed the point. Yet, what about us Christians, more especially those who are so-called full-time Christian servants? I think sometimes it is easier for us to miss the point than for those who are not "full-time" (even though every believer ought to be "full-time" for Christ), but you know what I mean.

Yet, there is the dire danger of our going through the motions of being "religious," carrying out the forms and churchly rituals, and finally reaching the end of our journey on a tragic discord—asking oneself, "Did I miss the point? Where did I go wrong? Have I been so busy 'serving' and making a living that I seldom thought about making a life?" My fervent prayer is that none of you will be confronted with this eleventh-hour shock.

Here is a classic illustration of what I have in mind. Wilbur and Orville Wright, on December 17, 1903, at Kitty Hawk, North Carolina, made the first successful heavier-than-air flight in history. Not a very long flight, its length was less than the wingspan of a modern B-52. Yet, it was a first.

In their ecstasy they rushed to the telegraph station where they sent a message to their sister in Dayton, Ohio. The telegram read: "First sustained flight, 59 seconds. Home for Christmas." Their sister, of course, was elated. With the message in hand, she ran all the way to the newspaper office.

Laying the message on the desk of the editor, she exclaimed, "I thought you would want to see this for tomorrow's paper." The paper came out, and buried on page 16 underneath the obituary column was the notice, "Local bicycle merchants to spend the holidays at home." Can you believe that? The editor missed the entire point of one of the greatest events in history.

Jesus, with broken heart, watched people doing that every day. The perceptive Christian has the same disheartening experience. And Jesus tried to warn His hearers, disciples and non-disciples, not to rush through every day losing out on the reality of life. So He related one illustrative story after another, fervently trying to lead His hearers away from lives of banality and emptiness.

One of His accounts was about the rich farmer. Isn't it sad that the notes in most Bibles and commentaries refer to this story as "the parable of the rich fool"? The fellow might have had a solid-sounding name like Jonathan or Aaron or Reuben or Joshua, but he has gone down in history as a "fool," albeit at one time a rich one (see Luke 12:16-21).

One commentator, Arthur John Gossip, believes the rich farmer probably lived down the road from Jesus, that Jesus had actually known the man. Of course, there is a sense in which Jesus knows every man and woman. The man was most successful, and there is no indication he was cruel, hateful, or negligent of the poor.

I can imagine that he walked out into his fields and viewed them with pride. Every country and small-town preacher has probably strolled through the fields with farmer members or prospects, listening to the farmer bragging about his crop and his livestock. The rich farmer began to muse to himself, *What am I gonna do with this bumper crop? I'll tell you what I'm gonna do. I'm gonna tear down these old barns and silos, and I'm gonna build bigger ones, and then I'll have enough room for all my produce.*

And I'm gonna sort of retire and live off the fat of the land. Gonna eat and drink and live it up.

But that night God came to him and called him a fool. Now you and I may not have the right to call someone a fool, but God does. For instance, "The fool hath said in his heart, There is no God" (Psalm 14:1, KJV).

"This night thy soul shall be required of thee . . ." But why? Not because he was prosperous. Not because he was an astute agribusinessman, not because he could build more spacious facilities. But because he swapped his entire life for that which can be stored behind a barn door.

Now, we can whisper "fool," but you and I can fall prey to the same pointless attitude. We can make the means to an end the end itself. Ask many young people and older, "What do you want out of life?" and they reply, with total disregard for the long look, "Oh, I want a better car, a Corvette or a Firebird or a Z-28. And I want a bigger house or apartment, plenty of money in the bank, vacations on the beach. And I want security. And I want to go where I want to go when I please." Not one mention of others, of values—of God.

Many of us Christians carry a twisted set of values and accentuate the wrong aspects of life. There is nothing wrong with a house, a car, a bit of money in the bank, security— provided you do not stop there. What will you do with those belongings?

When I was a kid in West Tennessee, living on the banks of the Forked Deer River, I was about the best marble shooter in Crockett County. I had a Bull Durham sack—you remember the kind with the strings—full of the most beautiful marbles you've ever seen. I'm not talking about "beanies"—I'm thinking of *glassies*. Now they remind me of miniature color photos of Jupiter and Saturn and Mars. Oh, those marbles were pretty.

There was a pal of mine who coveted my marbles. He was about two years older than I, but he couldn't win my marbles because I was a better shooter.

But he had a prized possession, a "good luck charm," a strange-looking doodad. Track and field was big in our curriculum at Alamo, Tennessee. As we would run down country roads, my friend would clasp that metal "thang" next to his heart, and he could beat all of us as long as he had his charm, so it seemed.

Once in a while he would let me borrow the "thang," and I could outrun him five or ten yards in the half-mile run. You guessed it. I traded him my sack full of glassies for his charm—and soon discovered that it was nothing but a piece of metal out of his mama's cook stove. Now you've found out how "I lost my marbles." But multitudes of folks are playing for keeps and losing not marbles, but their souls.

Hettie Green was affectionately known as "The Witch of Wall Street." She inherited six million dollars, but before she died she parlayed that into over one hundred million dollars. While she did she lived in squallor in one of the apartments in a tenement she owned. A virtual "bag woman," she roamed the alleys gathering newspapers, bottles, and rags before the rag man came to pick them up. She piled up the junk until the proper time for her to sell it.

One day her son, Ned, skinned his knee in a sledding accident. The knee became infected, but the miserly woman would not have it treated because of the money involved (and she was a multimillionaire!). Finally, the boy's condition worsened, and he had a high fever. One night she wrapped him in old rags, carried him to the hospital, and asked for charity treatment for her son. As the doctor was treating the boy, he recognized "The Witch of Wall Street," stopped the treatment, and demanded payment for his services—five whole dollars.

Hettie Green became indignant, ranting about money-grubbing doctors. She left the hospital without letting the doctor finish the treatment. The result: Ned's leg later had to be amputated—because of Hettie's sinful obsession. A multimillionaire who had missed the whole point of life God had given her and caused her son to be a cripple the rest of his life.

Why did Jesus continually warn about the inordinate love of money and possessions? Easy to see, isn't it?

> Lay not up for yourselves treasures upon earth, where moth and rust doth corrupt, and thieves break through and steal: But lay up for yourselves treasures in heaven, where neither moth nor rust doth corrupt, and where thieves do not break through nor steal: For where your treasure is, there will your heart be also. . . . No man can serve two masters: for either he will hate the one, and love the other; or else he will hold to the one, and despise the other. Ye cannot serve God and mammon (Matt. 6:19-21,24, KJV).

Put all of Jesus' teachings together, and you will be astonished at His stewardship content. Thirty-three years ago Merrill D. Moore wrote a classic stewardship book, *Found Faithful*. Concerning Jesus' teachings Moore (no kin except in Jesus) observed:

> Jesus took the idea of stewardship as found in Jewish and Roman life, and lifted it to express the relationship between God and man. Jesus was indicating by this figure that God is the Owner and man is the steward entrusted with the administration of the things God has committed to him for his use. . . . The larger portion of the recorded sayings of Jesus deal with property and the right use of it. He has more to say about stewardship than any other single theme which he discussed. It is said that one out of every

six verses in the Gospels deal with the theme. Any exhaustive study of what Jesus taught about stewardship will exceed the limits of this [study course] book.[1]

You and I are not immune to placing too much emphasis on the material side of our lives. As Christians we will sometimes cover up our selfishness with a facade of one kind or another. We excuse our preoccupation with "mammon" by thinking or actually verbalizing, *Well, you know, I've got to make a living. Have to take care of my family. Why, the Bible says if I don't, I'm worse than an infidel. So, I've got all these things going on the side, and I'm going to stash it away for the rainy day.*

I'm the first to admit I'm far from perfect, but my ministry has to come first. I know of so many "full-time Christian workers" who are obsessed with sideline financial interests to the extent that they neglect their ministry. There is nothing wrong with making honest money provided that money does not interfere with our service to the Lord "who giveth thee power to get wealth" (Deut. 8:18, KJV).

Do you know what one dollar bill is worth? Now, I am not touching on what inflation has done to the dollar. I mean a literal one dollar bill. It is worth one fifth of one penny! That's what it costs for the U.S. Government to manufacture one of them.

A few years ago I was in the Amarillo National Bank vault and actually held a ten thousand dollar bill in my hand. It's the only one I've ever seen. By now I reckon they trust me in Amarillo. Yet, a guard stood on either side of me.

Now, guess what it costs to make a ten thousand dollar bill. Exactly what it costs for the government to print a one dollar bill—two tenths or one fifth of one cent! Wouldn't it be pathetic for us to spend our entire lives seeking to acquire currency which has a set value assigned to it by our government or by the so-called World Bank?

But money is an appropriate jumping-off point for other urgent matters as well.

When I moved to Amarillo a quarter-century ago, the inner-city area was in the process of moving out to shopping centers and suburban areas. Our church is located in downtown Amarillo. I realized almost fearfully that if the church were to remain growing and vital in the inner city, we were going up against the mobility of the city. I thought to myself, *Moore, the church and you are going to have to do something fresh, different, unique if you're going to stay alive.*

One of my first impulses was to visit all of the mainline book stores and ask the clerks, "What are people buying in Amarillo?" How could I meet people's needs if I didn't know what they were reading and feeling and thinking?

Personal problems headed the list—fear, worry, anxiety, "nerves," and the like. I bought one of them, *You and Your Nerves,* and put it on the nightstand by the bed. One night before going to sleep I began to read it. That book made me so nervous I couldn't sleep the rest of the night!

The reading tastes of the public have hardly changed in twenty-five years—*Passages, Looking Out for Number One, How to Survive the Coming Economic Crunch, How to*

Avoid Probate—How to Cope . . ., How to Survive . . ., How to Make It . . ., on and on. The media plays on and profits from our fears and insecurities.

What is the cause of all these anxieties, tensions, and hang-ups? What is the matter with us that we are so insecure? Why is it that the highest suicide rate is between the ages of eighteen and twenty-two? Why is it so many people are broke from going to therapists and psychiatrists at fifty to one hundred dollars an hour? And I am not knocking ethical, qualified Christian counselors, please understand.

I believe with all of my heart the answer is this: persons have been cheapened in our day. That's happened in our churches, in our communities, in our nation. Our people—and I am one—have lost confidence in what we are and who we are. We are akin to the committee that the Israelites sent over into the Land of Promise. With the exception of Joshua and Caleb, the spies came back moaning the blues. It was a mixed report: "Why, everything's as grand as we've heard it was, but there are giants over there. We are like grasshoppers in their eyes.

And that's happened in our country—we have "The Grasshopper Syndrome." We feel so depersonalized and puny and insignificant, so we miss out on many promises of God. If we are saved, we will ultimately make the Promised Land, but think of all the joy-filled blessings we'll miss here.

Because of these feelings, we are almost afraid to be individuals of worth to do what God assigned us to do—"go up and take the land," instead of roaming around in the wilderness most of—or all of—our lives. Deep down inside there is a craving, a haunting yearning do to better, to move out for Christ . . . but . . .

Even in our churches, people often feel alienated and left-out. Sure, some people have a chip on their shoulder, and you can never please them. But there are many sincere souls who are genuinely hungry for brotherly and sisterly love. With all of my heart I challenge you to reevaluate yourself. You're not a grasshopper. You're a child of the King of kings and Lord of lords. The image of the Lord Jesus, in all of His beauty, is stamped upon your heart. You're supposed to be becoming more like Him, "more like the Master." Then, when you meet Him face to face, you're going to be like Him, "for we shall see him as he is" (see 1 John 3:2b, KJV).

We also are called on to place a new estimate of value on the people with whom we come in contact. Try not to look at what they are but what they could be for Christ.

One old preacher declared, "America is on a toboggan slide to hell." And that's the truth, but it's not enough to holler about our complex problems. Nearly every major problem facing this nation is because there is a lack of faith. This vacuum has caused a pall of pessimism to fall over this great land.

If we are not careful, you and I certainly relate to an incident shared by the late Bennett Cerf. While in the Midwest he picked up a county newspaper to read the weather report for the following day. In the weather report there was one word missing, and the report came out: "Less than a five percent chance of today and tomorrow." And we often feel it is coming down to sheer doom.

The answer is so plain, but we Christians are "at ease in Zion." We are existing in a spiritual limbo, robot-like going through the motions, "having a form of godliness but denying the power thereof."

We can expect those outside Christ to be all messed up and living by warped values, but all too many of us Christians are hardly any different. Like one country sage put it, "You can put us in a bag and shake us up and we come out looking pretty much alike." Many of our problems are caused by the very fact that we as Christians have not asserted our values before the world. We are so afraid to offend that we have become downright innocuous and have virtually no clout in society. So bit by bit the mores and values which helped build our country have eroded—and now there is an avalanche of the rock on which our nation was founded.

One of my friends from Topeka, Kansas, told me about going to Washington, D.C. He was staying with a friend of his in Georgetown in a townhouse. At six in the morning there was a loud knock at the door. Grabbing his robe, he answered the door, and there was his host standing there. "Would you help me?" the host implored. "Of course, I'll help you," the friend replied. The host handed a .12-gauge shotgun to my friend and requested, "Please cover me. I'm going out to get the morning paper!" When you come right down to it, that's not really funny.

We have majored on the problems to the extent that we have bypassed the greatest Problem Solver. We have actually forgotten that Jesus came to give us life and to give it more abundantly—yes, superabundantly.

A husband came home drunk. His patient wife had seen him in that condition so many times that she was fed up. "You're going to hell if you don't change your ways," she scolded. She calmed down and said, "Well, I really don't know about that, but you're going to the opera tonight, whether or not you want to." He decided he'd better go. They seated themselves in the front row of the balcony to watch the performance.

If you are familiar with the story, at one point in *Faust*, Satan goes back to hell, and he is to be followed by Faust. All was arranged. There was a trapdoor in the floor. At the appropriate moment, Satan dropped through the trapdoor, and Faust started to follow. But the singer playing Faust was rather rotund and could not negotiate the passage. He became stuck trying to go through the trapdoor. He was suspended—could not go down, could not go up. About that time the drunk fellow began to stir. When he groggily beheld the hilarious scene, with Faust being unable to descend, he jumped up, raised his hands, and yelled, "Fantastic, Mama, hell is full!"

Of course, we know hell is never full. "Hell and destruction are never full; so the eyes of man are never satisfied" (Prov. 27:20, KJV). But because of conditions around us, we sometimes think hell, like an old septic tank, is full and backing up on us. We become so enmeshed in problems that we lose our ability to enjoy life and share the abundant life of Christ with others.

We miss the point if we live only for ourselves, if we become ingrown with our pessimism and cynical about people out in the world. I beseech you not to become a Scrooge, a Silas Marner, a Hettie Green. Open up your heart and let the sunshine out—not in, as in the song of the mid-fifties. If you're a Christian, somewhere inside is the sunshine of God's love. Free it. Let it out.

You totally bypass the point Jesus makes if you live for yourself to the virtual exclusion of others.

You are familiar with Jacob and his favorite son, Joseph. As Jacob reached the end of his life, he came to a dreadful realization—he had missed the point in many respects. It was too late for Jacob to change the consequences of his past life.

Jacob had openly favored Joseph to the hurt and jealousy of Jacob's other sons. Jacob's malfeasances had been many. But he did not want Joseph to miss the point, so he prayed a special prayer for him. "God, grant Joseph a brave heart so he can face life unafraid, and give him a sense of Your presence continually with him."

There is the kind of prayer we should pray for our children. I do not care whether they are famous or wealthy. More than all else I want them to have the assurance as they reach the end of life, "I have done the will of God. I have lived for Him. Somehow I have done part of what He had for me to accomplish." It will justify my life if my children can make the most of the abundant life.

Dr. Walter Judd, former medical missionary and congressman, spoke at a Chamber of Commerce banquet in our city several years ago. He closed out his message with this experience.

Many years before, as Walter Judd was about to graduate from medical school, it became known to his professors and colleagues that he had surrendered his life to medical missions. They chided him in class about "wasting his life," and that hardly fazed him until his favorite professor called him in and lectured him, "Walter, I can't believe you're going to waste your life, your knowledge, and skill in some faraway place where they can't possibly appreciate what you can do!"

His professor continued, "You can set up an office in any city, and in a short time you can be independently wealthy. You can have friends, fame, and acclaim." But God had called Walter to the foreign mission field. Upon graduation he headed out for China as a missionary.

While on ship coming back to the states on his first furlough, Judd received a wire from that professor, stating, "As soon as you dock, I must see you at once. Please come to my home."

Although he did not understand, Judd went to the professor's home as soon as possible. They entered the study, away from their families. As they sat down, the professor began talking, "Walter, you know that I've never had but three ambitions in life. I wanted to be the best doctor I was capable of becoming. I really wanted to be a 'doctor's doctor'—the kind that other physicians and surgeons can send for when they were in difficulty, when they had problems."

In a torrent of words, the professor continued: "You know my reputation, how I've traveled all over this nation giving assistance to fellow physicians. I also wanted a fine family. You know my lovely wife and our fine children." On and on he went, "And I wanted an income that would let me provide for our family, the kind I thought they deserved to have.

"You see this well-appointed home. There is the lake, the swimming pool—all of it is paid for." But the professor dropped his head and blurted out, "Walter, tell me, what's wrong with me? Everything in life seems like sand slipping through my fingers. What's wrong?"

Judd said to that banquet, "I could have told him, but I simply did not have the heart. There was nothing wrong with a single ambition that doctor ever had, but no person can order his life just to live for himself and his own immediate circle". . . . without losing out and missing the whole point.

Brian Harbour tells of an account in a newspaper:

A small-town, weekly newspaper described the robbery and murder of a local businessman. He was waylaid after work on Saturday night on his way home. The newspaper article stated, "Fortunately for the deceased, he had just deposited his day's receipts in the bank, with the result that he lost nothing but his life!" Wasn't he fortunate?[2]

Whoever wrote the article probably did not mean it like it sounded, but it conveyed the predominant disregard for human life in our country. It sort of reminds you of Tom T. Hall's "Ballad of Forty Dollars." It's about a gravedigger who watches a man's interment and goes into considerable detail. At the end, the gravedigger laments, "Trouble is, he owed me forty bucks." In other words, it wasn't sad that the man died—only that he died without repaying a debt.

It is so apparent that the most important consideration is the life that Jesus Christ intended for us to have—our sins forgiven, a right relationship with God through the blood of the Lord Jesus, and here and now to have an abundant life. That implies the quality of life Jesus Christ demonstrated when He walked this earth in the incarnation.

Do you honestly have that quality of life? Do you? I pray to God that you do. He wants us to have that quality of life every moment of every hour of every day.

Decades ago, when Leo Tolstoy, the famed Russian author, was alive, a young artist asked the Christian count to critique a painting of the Last Supper. After studying it with care, Tolstoy pointed to Jesus in the center and remarked, "You do not love Him."

Puzzled, the artist asked, "Why, that is the Lord Jesus Christ."

"I know," answered the count, "but you do not love Him. If you did, you would paint Him better!"

> Christ, the Transforming Light,
> Touches this heart of mine,
> Piercing the darkest night,
> Making His glory shine.

Oh, to reflect His grace,
Causing the world to see,
Love that will glow
Till others shall know
Jesus revealed in me![3]
—Gipsy Smith

4

No One Is an Island

For none of us liveth to himself, and no man dieth to himself. For whether we live, we live unto the Lord; and whether we die, we die unto the Lord; whether we live therefore, or die, we are the Lord's. For to this end Christ hath died, and rose, and revived, that he might be Lord both of the dead and living.

Romans 14:7-9, KJV

John Donne, Christian poet whose life spanned the sixteenth and seventeenth centuries, is perhaps best-known for his statement: "No man is an island complete unto himself." That mystical English cleric was only articulating the truth of which Paul wrote in this passage of Scripture.

Verse 7 sums it up: "For none of us liveth to himself, and no man dieth to himself." This world is freighted with problems because unregenerate people have not realized and lived by this belief in interdependence.

You have discovered, as I have, that most every problem involves human relations. Most of the time when a business goes bankrupt or a person loses his job, it is not because they lacked expertise, savvy, or drive. Disaster often results because people simply cannot get along with others and vice versa.

Churches split. Some of them have to close down. Governments topple. Wars are fought. Because people cannot or will not exercise what Ernest White has called *The Art of Human Relations*.

Our Lord and Savior Jesus Christ, I am persuaded, is far more interested in how we relate to one another than how we interpret Ezekiel's wheels or the image in Daniel 2 or the exegesis of any particular book or mystery in God's fully inspired Word. How do you get along with your family, your coworkers, your boss, the service station attendant, the grocery checker, the pharmacist, your fellow church members, and others?

In addition to the text, only one verse is needed to demonstrate the first sentence of the previous paragraph. Jesus is personally involved in how we relate to others. Here it is:

And the King shall answer and say unto them, Verily I say unto you, Inasmuch as ye have done it unto one of the least of these my brethren, ye have done it unto me (Matt. 25:40, KJV).

What does that prove? That what we do for our fellow human beings, and how we treat them, is indicative of how we are ultimately treating God Almighty! Human beings, no matter how defiled and gross, no matter how filthy with sin, were created by the Heavenly Father. We cannot do good to another person without that good rising up before the Throne of God.

Conversely, when we sin against another person, we are

ultimately sinning against God. King David committed two heinous sins—adultery and murder. He lusted after Bathsheba, the beautiful wife of Uriah the Hittite. He then plotted Uriah's death, making himself an accomplice to the crime. He instructed Joab, in a letter delivered by Uriah himself, "Set ye Uriah in the forefront of the hottest battle, and retire ye from him, that he may be smitten, and die" (2 Sam. 11:15, KJV).

I referred to "two heinous sins." Actually, sin compounds itself. Examine 2 Samuel 11 and discover how "the sweet singer of Israel" evilly plotted and schemed against poor, unsuspecting Uriah. Add to the two sins these others: covetousness, cheating, lying, stealing, trickery, and downright meanness, and you have a crime which makes Watergate look like a seated tea for debutantes!

David then heard the thunderous condemnation from the Prophet Nathan, "Thou art the man" (2 Sam. 12:7, KJV). Many commentators feel that David never had a comfortable day the rest of his life.

One definite note is crystal-clear: David then understood the nature of sin. In his Penitential Psalm, 51, he wailed:

> For I acknowledge my trangressions: and my sin is ever before me. Against thee, thee only have I sinned, and done this evil in thy sight: that thou mightest be justified when thou speakest, and be clear when thou judgest (Ps. 51:3-4, KJV).

You cannot sin against man without it hurting God. Do good, and you have done that good to Jesus. Sin, and you have sinned against the Holy God of Glory.

So, human relations are immeasurably important to the Lord Jesus.

It's too bad that sometimes people outside the church show the need for one another more than we "insiders." They can come together in giant endeavors like "Live Aid" for the starving millions in Africa and "Farm Aid" for the struggling farmers of America.

And even many non-Christian songwriters compose songs about needing one another and love and caring and standing together.

First of all, we as Christians honestly need one another. Now, all of us are faced with those fussy days when we want to withdraw into a shell. I have to fight those feelings of "live and let live, and leave me alone while I do it." I guess even the most extroverted person wants to pull in his antennae once in a while. We often have a "hermit" complex and want to flee other human beings.

But upon a moment's reflection, we realize that withdrawal is unworkable—that none of us can live in isolation. I am reminded of George Fox's prayer: "O God, I pray to be baptized into a sense of all conditions that I might be able to know the needs and feel the sorrows of all men."

A friend of mine was waiting on the bus. His usual custom was to engage other prospective passengers in conversation, so he decided to talk with a rather unkempt fellow. My friend came around to the subject of Jesus, asking him, "Friend, wouldn't you like to have Jesus as your Lord and Savior?" The man adamantly replied, "Listen to me, I don't need nobody!" Several days later my friend was talking with another passenger and asked about the fellow who didn't need "nobody." The fellow passenger exclaimed, "Good grief, didn't you know? That man's as crazy as a Betsy bug!" What a commentary! Only a person who had taken leave of his senses would feel, "I don't need nobody!"

Envision the consequences of living without others. Death would come rather swiftly. After a while, no food. No communication. No medicine. No clean water. No provisions. No means of transportation. A person in total isolation would think of a thousand things he could not do for himself for a thousand different reasons.

You and I do need other people, for there is no success in total isolation. OK, but if we learn this lesson, we must also begin to seek and to cherish the friendship of others. That means to inject warmth into our friendship with others, not just a matter of enduring or putting up with other folks. As Christians we are called on to be lights which give illumination and to be salt which seasons.

If you are making friends for Jesus, people will say about you, "You light up my life." The Christian lights and seasons.

George Eliot aptly wrote:

> Every soul that touches yours—
> Be it the slightest contact—
> Get therefrom some good;
> Some little grace; one kindly thought;
> One aspiration yet unfelt;
> One bit of courage
> For the darkening sky;

One gleam of faith
To brave the thickening ills of life;
One glimpse of brighter skies—
To make this life worth while
And heaven a surer heritage.

All of us are innately selfish. In Christ we are moving away from self and selfishness, but it remains a struggle. At times we try to mask our selfishness, our egotism, but it seeps out like the telltale odor from a mildewed carpet. We put up a facade, and we use terminology trying to cover up how self-centered we are. Most of us do not go quite as far as the unmarried lady who prayed, "O Lord, I do not ask anything for myself, but please, Lord send my mother a son-in-law!"

We are tainted with self-concern. They used to call it "enlightened self-interest." We hope Mark Twain was jesting when he quipped, "Good breeding consists in concealing how much one thinks of self and how little he thinks of others."

In addition to injecting warmth into friendship, we must learn to respect the feelings of others. My older readers will remember Huey P. Long, "The Kingfish" who was governor of Louisiana in the 1930s. Long once stated there was a time when he tried to get things done by saying "please." But, according to Long, that did not work. So, in essence, he admitted, "I became a 'dynamiter.' I began to blast things and people out of my way in order to get things done." But the tables were turned. Mr. Long, while standing on the Capitol steps in Baton Rouge, was blasted out of this world by an assassin's bullets. The best-selling book, *How to Win Through Intimidation*, was off base. No one ultimately wins through intimidation or abusing the rights of others.

I have run into plenty of people who harp on law and order, so long as they lay down the law and give the order—but that's the only time they really believe in law and order.

We must learn to respect the feelings and rights of others, yet we need to exercise judgment in the matter. Maybe we at least ought to display the caution of the drunk who wandered into a Texas bar. He held a piece of paper in his hand. One of the patrons asked, "What you got on that sheet of paper?" The drunk answered, "This' a list of all the men in this town I can whip." A Texan who would make John Wayne look like a midget jumped off of the bar stool, stared down into the drunk's beady little eyes, and menacingly asked, "Boy, is my name on that list?" "I don't know. I'll look and see," came the answer.

"Yep, here's your name right here."

"You snake, you can't whip me. No way in the world."

The inebriated one replied, "All right, I'll take your name off the list then."

Leaving that aside, if only we could live by what is commonly called "The Golden Rule." Jesus taught in His Sermon on the Mount:

> Therefore all things whatsoever ye would that men should do to you, do ye even so to them: for this is the law and the prophets (Matt. 7:12, KJV).

Slice it however you wish. Paraphrase it "do unto others as you would have them do unto you." Many seem to twist it to mean "Do others" or "do unto others" before they do it to you. Beat them to the punch.

> Likewise God's children are to do good things to others. Jesus put the sum of the law and the prophets into the statement we call the Golden Rule: "Whatever you wish that men would do to you, do so to them" (v. 12). This saying was already known to the Jews in negative form. His followers were not simply to keep from doing to another that which they did not want done to themselves. Jesus changed it into positive, active form. They were to treat others in the same way they would like for others to treat them.[1]

And we must also learn how not to project our problems onto other people. "How are you?" is a greeting, not an invitation. And there are multitudes of folks I would never ask, "How are you?" Unless I had at least an hour to listen to an organ recital—because they will recite every organ in their bodies that is not functioning properly. So, remember that you do not always have to be "Mr." or "Mrs. Right." Neither do you need to dump all of your problems on others. Most folks already have more than enough problems.

Sometimes you may have to answer, "Ok. Swell. Great," even though you may have one foot in the grave. But you may remonstrate, "You know, you'd be lying if you were about to croak and you answered, 'I'm fine. I'm great.'" If you are a Christian and about to drop dead, that is fine. In fact, that is stupendous, because you are headed for heaven. So go ahead and respond like that—you'll feel better, and they'll certainly appreciate your response.

I'm not nearly through. Let me suggest that we need to

learn how to overlook the faults of others. Along that line we must stand ready to forgive others.

The Book is chock-full of wisdom about faultfinding and forgiveness:

> And be ye kind one to another, tenderhearted, forgiving one another, even as God for Christ's sake hath forgiven you (Eph. 4:32, KJV).

> And forgive us our debts as we forgive our debtors (Matt. 6:12, KJV).

> For if ye forgive men their trespasses, your heavenly Father will also forgive you: But if ye forgive not men their trespasses, neither will your Father forgive your trespasses (Matt. 6:14-15, KJV).

> Confess your faults one to another, and pray one for another, that ye may be healed (James 5:16*a*, KJV).

> Brethren, if a man be overtaken in a fault, ye which are spiritual, restore such an one in the spirit of meekness; considering thyself, lest thou also be tempted (Gal. 6:1, KJV).

> Judge not, that ye be not judged (Matt. 7:1, KJV).

Thomas á Kempis advised, "Be not angry that you cannot make others as you would have them to be, seeing you cannot even make yourself as you want to be." If only we could remember his ancient admonition, we would learn how to overlook the faults of those around us. None of us are qualified to find fault. We have sin and therefore cannot cast a stone. Remember Jesus and His encounter with the woman caught in the very act of adultery. Her accusers could not cast a stone—one by one they disappeared. Jesus was the only One qualified to find fault and to cast a stone. Of course, He did not and would not. He sent the repentant former adulteress away with words of comforting forgiveness. "Neither do I condemn thee: go, and sin no more" (John 8:11, KJV).

What a difference it would make if, knowing full well we are faulty, we would quit our faultfinding as though we were divine. Perhaps drama, literary, and music critics are necessary, but they must have a wizened experience being paid to nitpick. It is a shame that one bad review from a critic can close down a good play or musical. I wonder how may people turn out for a critic's funeral.

John Ruskin, the famed painter and author, defined a critic as "one who cannot paint." Bravo. And Henry Ward Beecher once commented, "Every man should keep a fair-sized cemetery in which to bury the faults of his friends."

I dearly love the story of the little girl who came home from school with her notebook already graded by the teacher. And as little girls are inclined to do, she climbed into her daddy's lap to show him the notebook. As she turned the pages, big red As appeared in the right-hand corners. Beaming, she would look into her father's face for approval.

Finally she came to a page not quite as neat, and there was no big red A there. Her pen had leaked, and there were two messy ink blots on the page. Hurriedly she put down two stubby fingers—one to cover one blot and the other to cover the second. With Shirley Temple innocence she gazed into her father's face and begged, "Daddy, please don't see the blots!"

All of my life I've been saying that to the people I know. "Please don't see the blots. They're there, and I am painfully aware of them. I've seen them again and again, and I am far more familiar with them than you will ever be. Please don't see them!"

But if I ask you not to see the blots, I must be willing to look at you, not overlooking the blots but not even seeing them at all. If we want to master the art of human relations, we need to overlook the faults and flaws of others.

Yet, there is another ingredient which helps us in our relationships—a tremendous sense of humor. It still remains, "A merry heart doeth good like a medicine: but a broken spirit drieth the bones" (Prov. 17:22, KJV). Beware of those who have no sense of humor and never seem to laugh.

Where I live I probably receive more anonymous mail than the governor of the state. It's amazing why people write to me. They may not like what the governor or the president have done, so they write me as though they were blaming me. About a half dozen folks write most of the letters. I've learned to recognize them and don't even read them. But I am writing a book entitled *How to Write Anonymous Letters*. (I hope Broadman will publish it.) When you see it on the book store shelf, buy it because it is going to contain some of the juiciest morsels you have ever read.

Henry Ward Beecher, whom I have already quoted, used to receive loads of anonymous mail. One day he opened an anonymous goodie. Right in the middle of the page was one word: "Fool." Beecher carried the letter to the pulpit the following Sunday. He stood up and read the one-word letter to the congregation. "Folks," he announced. "I have often heard of a person writing a letter and 'forgetting' to sign his name. But this is the first time I have received one where the person signed his name and forgot to write the letter." A good sense of humor will save the day quite often.

Innumerable humorless people are spending "big bucks" on psychiatrists' couches when the habit of laughter might well heal their emotions. The Christian is really the only person who has a justification for laughter. He ought to laugh all the way to heaven. Jesus has made it possible. It reminds me of the little chorus, "I've got the joy, joy, joy, joy down in my heart, down in my heart, down in my heart. I have the love of Jesus down in my heart, down in my heart to stay."

S. Hall Young wrote:

> Let me die, laughing.
> No sighing o'er past sins; they are forgiven.
> Spilled on this earth are all the joys of heaven.

And the Christian ought to live laughing—and die laughing.

In relating to others, we must learn somehow to appreciate the best in them. It is not enough merely to overlook faults and frailties. We need to go beyond that and look for the good characteristics and traits in them. Ralph Waldo Emerson expressed it well: "We must be as courteous to a person as we are to a picture which we are always willing to hang in the best light."

Have we thought about how to put all of our friends—and even some of our enemies—in the best light? Why is it the majority of people tend to accentuate the negative, not the positive? Isn't it often because we try to cover the bad within our lives by looking for it in others? That is the mind-set of the backbiter and the captious critic.

Maybe you are talking back to me, "Hmmm, I know some people who are so lousy and mean, there's just nothing good about them." Keep on trying. No telling, one tiny smidgin of good may come out somewhere. It's a cinch that if we look for the bad, we'll surely find it.

Paul could "lay the axe to the tree" when he needed to, but basically he looked for the good. He disagreed with Barnabas over young John Mark, who defected during the first missionary journey, but later restored John Mark (see Col. 4:10; Phil. 24; 2 Tim. 4:11). One of Paul's major emphases was edifying the saints. That means building them up, helping them to grow in the Lord, and looking for their positive points.

As God gives you grace, find something good about everybody, if you can—your workers and coworkers, your friends, your acquaintances, your family. Isaiah perceptively wrote: "The Lord God hath given me the tongue of the learned, that I should know how to speak a word in season to him that is weary . . ." (50:4, KJV).

Only eternity will tell what kind words, brief messages of encouragement, will mean to another's spirit—and to yours. A timely word may make a person's day, maybe even his month, and (who knows?) maybe even his life.

Robert Burns as a lad was cleaning up tables in an inn. One day he spilled a tray and was sorely reprimanded in public by his boss. But Sir Walter Scott called the boy aside and spoke words of comfort and encouragement. He asked the boy what he wanted to do with his life, to which Burns replied, "a writer, Sir." Throughout his life, the former busboy testified that Sir Walter Scott, a writing genius, turned his life around. If only someone had done that with another writer a few years back. The young man received one rejection slip after another. In his despondency, feeling the darkest depression, the fellow committed suicide. After his death, his mother had his novel published. Entitled *A Conspiracy of Dunces*, it became a best-seller. But the author was not around to enjoy the acclaim and positive reviews.

"For none of us liveth to himself, and no man dieth to himself," observed Paul. Shakespeare also expressed it: "Every man's death diminishes me."

And Paul also commanded the Galatians, and us, "Bear ye one another's burdens, and so fulfill the law of Christ" (6:2, KJV). Practice the Golden Rule. Live it out. Fleshen out the gospel in your daily life. Maybe you have become tired of hearing the oft-used phrase, "He ain't heavy. He's my brother." Regardless, it surely is fitting. That should be our attitude as we bear one another's burden's. "He ain't heavy. He's my brother." "She's my sister."

Frankly, you will encounter a few people who are human porcupines. You'll get stuck if you come close to them. The fact is—they don't want you close to them. They might as well hang a sign around their necks reading: DANGER

ZONE. KEEP YOUR DISTANCE. Many of them are born like that, and it sometimes seems there is nothing they can do about it. Try to break through but finally back away if you have to out of deference to them. You will discover that in many cases "misery *does not* love company." Stay away after you have exhausted all avenues of communication.

All of us can probably think of people we would rather not hang around, so we spend a minimum of time with them—the non-stop talkers, the chronic gripers, the inveterate gossips, and the poor martyrs. If they're going to be miserable, and there's nothing you or I can do to diminish their misery, we might as well let them "enjoy" their misery by themselves.

Jesus, the perfect Son of God, was not especially happy around the scribes and Pharisees, the lawyers from the synagogues, and the so-called religious hierarchy of the day. And he was roundly criticized because of the people with whom he associated—the publicans, the people of the streets, fishermen, farmers, and generally the common folks.

At our morning service, which is televised, I interview one five-year-old child. A five-year old can teach you plenty—and they can teach you in a hurry. Before we go out into the service I visit with the child I am going to interview. One particular Sunday a cute little girl who was to be interviewed by me on camera did not tell me in the office what she had in mind for me "live." Suddenly she asked, "Dr. Moore, would you like for me to tell you a joke?" Now, I have to confess that a joke from a five-year-old on television was not especially thrilling, considering what kids that age can come up with (remember Art Linkletter's *Kids Say the Darndest Things*).

But like the hypocrite I am, I smiled and answered: "Yes, darling," because you know what's going to happen if you answer in front of all those people, "No, honey, I don't want to hear your joke." Friend, you might as well close shop. You are out of business for sure.

She launched into her joke. "Did you hear about the room where there were four people, one in each corner and in the middle of the room was a hundred-dollar bill?"

"No, sweetheart," I answered nervously.

"Well," she continued, "in one corner was Santa Claus, and in one corner was the Easter Bunny. In another corner was a smart Aggie (student from Texas A & M), and in the other corner was a dumb Aggie. Do you want to know who got the hundred-dollar bill?"

Trembling, I replied, "Yes, dear."

"The dumb Aggie? Do you want to know why?" I nodded. "Because there is no Santa Claus, and there is no Easter Bunny, and there is no smart Aggie." We made friends with everybody that day—except the Aggies.

As I was about to wind up the interview with the little comedienne, a handsome kid kept pushing up against me, and he was trying to grab the microphone. Finally I asked, "Do you have something to say to the people?" to which he replied, "Yes, sir."

He took the mike and almost put it in his mouth like an ice

cream cone, announcing, "People, live it up." I believe he preached the best sermon they heard that day.

As God's people, *together* we need to "live it up" for Christ. We can begin to take ourselves too seriously, going through life in the subjunctive mood and the passive voice. Somehow many of us have never conveyed to the world that there is "joy, wonderful joy" when Jesus comes into the heart. Many people think of Christians as those who have pulled behind a chain-link fence so they can growl at the rest of the world as it passes by.

Isolationism, which helped lead to the Second World War, is dangerous in international diplomacy. And it is even more deadly in Christianity—because the eternal destinies of human beings are at stake. Yes, we are in the world but not of the world. Yes, we are a "peculiar people." There is a definite difference. Yet, we have a function, a role for God that no one else can fill. We are going to have to come out from behind the fences and emerge from our comfortable cloisters, and we are going to have to make an impact in a workaday world.

Life is like radar. You and I will receive from it exactly what we send out. As Christians it is not really what other people send out to us that we get. Try sending out good-will, kindness, love, smiles—and as surely as the sun came up this morning, it's going to come back. There's a sentimental old song which goes: "Give to the world the best you have, and the best will come back to you." And the late Frank Parker, tenor star of the 1920s and 1930s, made a brief comeback on *The Tonight Show* in its early days when Jack Parr was the host. Again and again Jack asked Frank to warble the song "Make Someone Happy." It ends, "Make someone happy, and you'll be happy, too."

If we send out ill will, growls, and grunts, they will boomerang on us. Jesus designed that principle.

> Give, and it shall be given you; good measure, pressed down, and shaken together, and running over, shall men give into your bosom. For with the same measure that ye mete withal it shall be measured to you again (Luke 6:38, KJV).

Jesus is not mainly referring to money but to all of life. Give, not because you expect to get—but if you give, you will get anyhow.

"No one is an island complete unto himself or herself." We need one another, and they need us. We are people who need people.

> How do you share the love of Jesus with
>   a lonely man?
> How do you tell a hungry man about the
>   Bread of Life?
>
> How do you tell a dying man about eternal life?
> How do you tell an orphan child about the
>   Father's love?
>
> How do you tell a loveless world that God
>   Himself is love?
> How do you help a man who's down to lift
>   His eyes above?

People who know go to people who need
 to know Jesus;
People who love go to people alone
 without Jesus;

For there are people who need to see,
 people who need to love,
 people who need to know God's redeeming
 love.

People who see go to those who are blind
 without Jesus,
And this is people to people, yes,
 people to people,
All sharing together God's love.[2]

5

What the Church Is

These things write I unto thee, hoping to come unto thee shortly: But if I tarry long, that thou oughtest to behave thyself in the house of God, which is the church of the living God, the pillar and ground of the truth.

1 Timothy 3:14-15, KJV

Were you aware that Albert Einstein, though an avowed Jew, was an admirer of the church of the Lord Jesus Christ? I quote Einstein, the physicist best known for "The Theory of Relativity":

Being a lover of freedom, when the revolution came in Germany, I looked to the universities to defend it [freedom], knowing that they had always boasted of their devotion to the cause of truth. But no, the universities immediately were silenced. Then I looked to the great editors in days gone by who proclaimed their love of freedom; but they, like the universities, were silenced within a few short weeks. Only the Church stood squarely across the path of Hitler's campaign for the supression of truth. I never had any special interest in the Church before, but now I feel a great affection and admiration because the Church alone had the courage and persistence to stand for intellectual truth and moral freedom. I am forced thus to confess what I once despised I now praise unreservedly.[1]

The church is the only institution founded by the Lord Jesus Christ. He bought it with His blood. He sustains it with the power of the Holy Spirit. He commissions us to carry His message through the church. He declares that the gates of hell shall not prevail against it.

The church to many of us is what it became when we were growing up. Of course, there are exceptions, for instance those who started attending church in adulthood. Let me reminisce for a moment.

My church life began with the Methodists and the folks in the Quincy Methodist Church out in the country. My Sunday School teacher, Mrs. Speer, and the pastor, Brother Boatwright, are among those who gave me the opportunity of attending college during the Great Depression. They certainly knew tremendously more about theology than they did music, because they gave me a music scholarship! Would you believe it?

My Baptist upbringings were in the Bible Belt at a time when the influence of J. R. Graves was exceedingly strong. And in that section of the South, the voices of preachers like M. E. Dodd, R. G. Lee, and my college pastor, Dr. R. E. Guy, carried considerable weight. The Bible was believed from cover to cover, as it should be. And in the churches they either bitterly despised or passionately loved. More than all else, my godly mother taught me to love and have confidence in the church, from the first one I pastored in the country, which met in a school building, to the one I have now pastored for over a quarter of a century.

Because of my love for the Lord Jesus Christ and the church He established, it pains me when people deemphasize the church. It is not even necessary for me to mention that many professing Christians have practically nothing to do with a local church. Millions of our own Southern Baptists we are not even able to locate. They have become "the lost tribes of the SBC." Many are non-resident, and most of them are probably non-participatory—and many of them are dead physically. Quite a few are dead spiritually but still alive physically!

With far too many there is an absolute absence of interest in or love for the church. But when you come to the New Testament, there is an entirely different atmosphere.

And hath put all things under his feet, and gave him to be the head over all things to the church, Which is his body, the fullness of him that filleth all in all (Eph. 1:22-23, KJV).

For the husband is the head of the wife, even as Christ is the head of the church: and he is the saviour of the body. Therefore as the church is subject to Christ, so let the wives be to their own husbands in every thing. Husbands, love your wives, even as Christ loved the church, and gave himself for it (Eph. 5:23-25, KJV).

And he is the head of the body, the church: who is the beginning, the firstborn from the dead; that in all things he might have the preeminence . . . Who now rejoice in my sufferings for you, and fill up that which is behind of the afflictions of Christ in my flesh for his body's sake, which is the church (Col. 1:18-19,24, KJV).

We Baptists have been so afraid of the teaching that one must join the local church to be saved, we have gone too far to the opposite extreme. Many of us have deemphasized the church, and for that reason (that is one of them), our baptisms have drastically declined in our Convention. Now, the fact is: if a person is truly saved, he will belong to the body of Christ, whether or not he has yet submitted to water baptism. But more and more I am coming to the place where I believe: if a person truly has the Lord Jesus Christ, he will want to unite with the church in a local sense and be buried with the Lord in baptism. The born-again believer will want to identify with a body of God's believers.

"Christ loved the church and gave himself for it." Christ died for whom? A civic club, a lodge, a para-church group that gathers as a "mutual admiration society?" No. CHRIST DIED FOR THE CHURCH!

Let me continue the text in Ephesians 5: "Christ loved the church, and gave himself for it." That what?

That he might sanctify and cleanse it with the washing of water by the Word, That he might present it to himself a glorious church, not having spot, or wrinkle, or any such thing; but that it should be holy and without blemish (vv. 26-27, KJV).

Does that sound like the New Testament soft-pedaled the church? People who play down the role of the church in the eternal plan of God simply are not New Testament Christians!

Paul spoke of two loyalties in his life. "I speak concerning Christ and His church" (Eph. 5:32). People who dodge the church and disparage the church and denigrate the church are worlds away from the plain teachings of Paul about the church of the Lord Jesus Christ. The church is God's instrument by which His redeeming message is carried to the ends of the earth.

I am a friend to mankind. To the man who prizes sanity, peacefulness, pure-mindedness, and longevity, I am a necessity.

I am hung about with sweet memories—memories of brides, memories of mothers, memories of boys and girls, memories of the aged as they advance in years.

I am decked with loving tears, crowned by loving hands and hearts.

In the minds of the greatest persons on earth, I find a constant dwelling place. I live in the lives of the young and in the dreams of the old.

I safeguard humanity, with a friendly hand for the person in fine clothing and the fellow in rags.

I am the essence of good fellowship, friendliness, and love.

I have gifts that gold cannot buy, nor kings take away. They are given freely to all who ask.

I bring back the freshness of life, the eagerness, the spirit of youth, which feels it has something to live for.

I meet you with outstretched arms and with songs of gladness.

Some time—some day—in the near or far future, you may yearn for the touch of my hand.

I am a comforter and friend.

On behalf of Jesus Christ, I am calling you!

I AM THE CHURCH.[2]

If we are to witness with effectiveness, we must remember what the church is, what it stands for, and also what causes people to avoid it. Why do so many people express indifference toward it? Why do they either hate the church or seem to have no opinion at all? Why are so many becoming attached to para-church "fellowships" where people simply "drop in." Many people are spiritual vagabonds with no roots in a church. If they attend services, it is often with no sense of attachment. They are spectators and do not want to become involved. Springing up all over the land are various groups having no ties with other professing Christians and often turning into cults of personality. Droves of these spiritual vagabonds believe the last teachings they have heard, no matter how far-fetched.

Radio and television services offer convenient, accessible avenues for hearing the gospel, but they are no substitute for *being present* with the saints of God. The writer of Hebrews admonished his readers not to forsake the assembling of themselves together, as the manner of some was (see Heb. 10:25). There is nothing to compare with being personally involved in the activities and services of a Bible-believing, gospel-preaching church. Now, I fully recognize that for sickness and providential hindrance, many are unable to attend in person.

In our text Paul was asking Timothy to convey a message about the church. The believers were passing through troublesome times. So, he encouraged Timothy, his "son in the ministry," and those with whom Timothy would share the letter, to take courage. How could they do that? By being reminded of what the church is and why it exists.

Paul exuberantly calls it "the church of the living God." It is no mere human organism set up for secular or social ends. It is God's own church in which he dwells. The King James Version of our text uses "the church of the living God, the pillar and ground of the truth." *The New American Standard* states almost the same—"the pillar and support of the truth." Other translations variously render the word base or support as "bulwark," "foundation," or "substructure." Christ is the superstructure.

Every statement of faith would be woefully incomplete and sadly lacking without a declaration of loyalty to the church of the living God. I have never seen a statement of faith, a confession, or a creed without a clause concerning the church. How could they not when the New Testament is filled with the exaltation of the Lord Jesus Christ and His body, the church? The New Testament writers, moved by the Holy Spirit, have two subjects of supreme importance: 1. CHRIST 2. HIS CHURCH.

"Thou art the Christ, the Son of the living God" (Matt. 16:16, KJV). Notice the parallel there. Christ is the Son of the living God—in our text the church is "of the living God." "Upon this rock I will build my church; and the gates of hell shall not prevail against it," Jesus declared at Caesarea Philippi. From that moment until His death on the cross, Jesus gave Himself to building, teaching, and perfecting His church.

To Paul there is one institution commanding and glorious—the church. Paul, formerly Saul, made havoc of the church before His saving experience with the Lord Jesus. Acts 9 describes his old condition: "Now Saul, still breathing out threats and murder against the disciples of the Lord, went to the high priest, and asked for letters from him to the synagogues at Damascus, so that if he found any belonging to the Way, both men and women, he might bring them bound to Jerusalem" (vv. 1-2).

Again and again Paul testified how he had persecuted the church of God. In Acts 26, in the presence of King Agrippa, Paul confessed: "So then, I thought I had to do many things hostile to the name of Jesus of Nazareth. And this is just what I did in Jerusalem; not only did I lock up many of the saints in prisons, having received authority from the chief priests, but also when they were being put to death, I cast my vote against them. And as I punished them often in all the synagogues, I tried to force them to blaspheme; and being furiously enraged at them, I kept pursuing them even to foreign cities" (vv. 9-11).

In Galatians 1, Paul defended his ministry for Christ, which was often questioned by Christians who had remembered the old Saul, the Christ hater and persecutor of the church:

> For I would have you know, brethren, that the gospel which was preached by me is not according to man. For I neither received it from man, nor was I taught it, but I received it through a revelation of Jesus Christ. For you have heard of my former manner of life in Judaism, how I used

to persecute the church of God beyond measure, and tried to destroy it (vv. 11-13).

When Jesus came into Paul's life on the road to Damascus, he did a complete about face. He then loved the very church of God which he had once viciously hated and sought to annihilate.

Paul, through the Spirit, combed the Greek language to express his newfound love. He used metaphors rich enough to convey the importance and the primacy of the church— "family," "the temple," "the Bride," "the pillar and ground of truth."

The church is God's chosen medium of revelation. It is the instrument founded and chosen by Christ to carry the good news of the Gospel, that Jesus saves "unto the uttermost." In the Book of Revelation, one of the most beautiful pictures is that of the wedding of Christ and His Bride, the Church, and the great wedding feast which follows.

Today there is a vast difference. The question often heard is, "What's the use of the church?" We also are assailed with, "Other groups can do it better—at less cost—with less organization and machinery." Or, "let the church be the church," sometimes actually meaning, "Let the church be nothing!"

Yes, let the church be the church for every disgruntled, self-serving, misfit group that doesn't like gearing up for Gospel conquest. There are many who cry against the church. Yet, in spite of their derisive cries, nowhere else can people work together without some semblance of order. To live there must be a body, an organism, and that body must be organized to function. Some of these same people end up setting up their own organizations in an attempt to point out directions for all churches to take. Many detractors espouse, "Never let the church sound the alarm. Don't mention such in the house of God. Never let the church blow the trumpet of patriotism or love for and pride in our nation," which, with all its faults, is still the land of the free and the home of the brave.

Paul loudly proclaimed, "The Church is the pillar and the bulwark of the truth." Therefore, let me suggest that we let the church be more than a mausoleum or a "wet-nurse."

The church should "sound off" on the issues of the day. If some church bodies think America is as guilty as Communist Russia or Vietnam or Cambodia or Libya or Iran, then let those groups say so. If some bodies believe that every soldier who fought in our wars or military actions is a killer, and undeserving of respect or honor; that those who went to war to avoid another Poland, Pearl Harbor, or Vietnam, and are no more worthy of our prayers and support than those who made the hell of Korea, Vietnam, or Iran; then let those groups loudly so proclaim—and do all they can to weaken the nation's military will and might, so they can have another blood bath in the near future. *But they shall not have my vote or voice!*

Let the real church be something and never forget what she is—"the pillar and ground of the truth!"

Is it possible that many professing Christians have betrayed our own cause, "having a form of godliness but deny ing the power thereof"? Democracy and Christianity must not be identified as one and the same, and yet the roots of modern democracy lie in the government of the New Testament church. There is a striking similarity in what the two have been scuttled by—treachery within. In democracies we are familiar with the "fifth columnist" who made noteworthy contributions to the defeat and downfall of governments. In Christianity defeats can be traced to unChristian "Christians" in high and low places.

The lack of genuine statesmanship—along with the influx of gutter ethics and the exhibition of petty selfishness on the part of certain leaders of democracies—is fully matched by the present mediocrity among Christian leaders in their craving for prestige, praise, and power.

The citizens' indifference to the duties of citizenship is matched in Christianity by the apathy of members toward the obligations of church membership.

To witness today, we must become less concerned about who receives credit for what. It does not matter who does what, so long as God gets the glory. We must bear witness to Jesus Christ and His church.

Jesus promised the abiding presence of the Holy Spirit:

> But when the Comforter is come, whom I will send unto you from the Father, even the Spirit of truth, which proceedeth from the Father, he shall testify [bear witness of] me: And ye shall also bear witness, because ye have been with me from the beginning (John 15:26-27, KJV).

We ought to learn more and more about the Holy Spirit. The reason we know so little about Jesus is that we have not allowed the Holy Spirit to illumine us and to guide us in our interpretation of God's fully reliable Word.

A. J. Gossip relates this experience:

Years ago in Glasgow I was hurrying to a meeting in a distant part of the city one Sunday morning before the (street) cars began, and noticed what was then quite a new thing, the pavements chalked at intervals with invitations to a hall. I stopped a policeman and asked what it meant. "These are socialists," he said, "and since very early morning they have been out and about, inviting the whole universe to a little place that will hold scarcely anyone. Believe me, sir, I disagree with them, but men so much in earnest as they are, are sure one day to sweep the city. What can hold them? What can keep them down?" and then he added, "Why are you ministers not out and at it too? You have a case far better and more glorious. If you would only work for it as these men do for theirs, why, you would sweep the world."

James Black once observed, "I fear nothing so much as the 'clever minister.' Amid all life's agonies and sorrows, he is not only a tragic misfit, but a cruel irony."

The church, because she is the church, makes herself of no reputation and takes the form of a servant, willing to be found in likeness to her Master. When people criticize the church for her failures, for her hypocrites within, let them! In our communities where many doors open only to those whose wallet is full, to those who have five talents, to those who have position, to those who have rank and station, the church invites any and all to come and be saved, to come and grow, to come and serve—and ultimately to sit down at the banquet table of the King. The glory of the church is unique; surrounded by thousands of organizations and movements, she is unlike any one of them. She does not ask, "How much money?" "What kind of education?" "What is your place or business in society?" There is no question about influence or prestige—just "do you want to be a new person in Christ?"

The church does not open her doors just to "the beautiful people," the cultured, the rich, and the powerful. She invites little children, taking the risk of future transgressions. She invites the ignorant and unlearned, and agrees to teach them. She even invites the crude and the rude, accepts them, and attempts to complete their lives in Christ Jesus.

Nearly always, where there is a club or para-group, they do not summon, "Ho, everyone that thirsteth, come." They proclaim, "Ho, everyone with money, with position, with standing, come and we will give you the advantages you cannot afford to live without."

The church is in the world to do for the world what it cannot do for itself, and to present to the world what it most sorely needs—the glad news of God.

Yes, we face difficulties, we have serious problems, but the church has had them since New Testament days. All you have to do is read the Epistles. We often hear talk like this, "If only we could be like the New Testament church." That sounds fantastic on the surface, but who would want to transfer his letter to the church at Corinth? They were divided into camps or cliques—those who adhered to Paul, to Apollos, to Cephas (or Peter). Those were their three favorite preachers. One of the church leaders was living in incest with his mother or mother-in-law. They squabbled over the gifts of the Spirit, and there was discrimination because of social class. Every church in the New Testament had dilemmas and problems, but there was a core of caring, truly born-again believers who kept on keeping on.

Jesus made it plain that if the world hated Him, it would hate His disciples. The world will key in on the faults of believers. Throughout the centuries the church has had numbers of the faint-hearted who have trembled for the church. The enemies of the church have chortled, "Aha, they are going to be finished. Kaput." But the church continues to live and survive and carry the message of the Lord Jesus. As He was hanging on the cross, His detractors also thought He was finished. The Lord Jesus burst the bonds of death, and He is alive forevermore, the Son of the living God. And His church is the church of the living God!

Disaster could have befallen the early church, but they had received an unction from the Spirit of God. They could have fled in terror from the hostile religious persecutors of the establishment. They could have hid from the juggernaut of the Roman eagle. But what would have been more convenient and more deadly still, they could have been split apart by argument and division. Instead, they obeyed and prayed and waited together until the power of God fell upon them.

What could have happened did not happen. What apparently could not happen did happen. They turned the tables on the ungodly system of the day, and they outthought, outlived, and outdied the pagan world. Why were they willing to live for Jesus and also to die for him? Because they had felt the touch of Jesus' hand and had seen the miraculous power of the Almighty.

We have a message to deliver. If it is to be effective, it must be given under pressure, the pressure of the world's need, the pressure of our loyalty to Jesus, and the pressure of our experience of what we owe Him. All over the place we hear multitudes of people complaining, "The pressure's killing us!" The truth is: if you are not under pressure, you are dead already.

Let us call on people to give. Surely no one has a right to the church who has not decided to make as the principle of his/her life, "It is more blessed to give than to receive." God so loved the world that He gave His only begotten Son. If the Son is our Savior, we are by the new nature, givers. And the church must carry this appeal to the nth degree.

Giuseppe Garibaldi, the founder of modern Italy, challenged his troops: "Men, I have not called you to pleasure. If you go with me, you will not have an easy time. I cannot promise you wealth or comfort. No, I call you to war, to long marches, to hunger and weariness, to discomforts a thousand fold, to fighting, and even to death. Will you come with me on these terms for your country's sake?"

Christ's call is infinitely more challenging and pressurized. "If any man will come after me, let him deny himself, and take up his cross and follow me."

Today there is the emphasis on the Spirit-filled church, and I look to see evidence of that fullness in their love, fellowship, service, and Christlikeness. From many I observe those qualities, those manifestations of being filled with the Spirit. From some I see practically nothing and hear only an unintelligible sound. May we remember that the Spirit-filled church will be like the Spirit Who fills it!

We belong to "the church of the living God, the pillar and ground of the truth."

In our churches may we reaffirm the stately hymn of Sabine Baring-Gould:

> Onward, Christian soldiers!
> Marching as to war,
> With the cross of Jesus
> Going on before.
> Christ the royal Master,
> Leads against the foe;
> Forward into battle, See His banner
> go!
>
> Like a mighty army
> Moves the Church of God;
> Brothers, we are treading
> Where the saints have trod;
> We are not divided; All one body we,
> One in hope and doctrine, One in
> charity.
>
> Onward, Christian soldiers,
> Marching as to war,
> With the cross of Jesus
> Going on before!

6

Should We Be Here?

And six days later Jesus took with Him Peter and James and John his brother, and brought them up to a high mountain by themselves. And He was transfigured before them; and His face shone like the sun, and His garments became as white as light. And behold Moses and Elijah appeared to them, talking with Him. And Peter answered and said to Jesus, "Lord, it is good for us to be here; if You wish, I will make three tabernacles here, one for You, and one for Moses, and one for Elijah." While he was still speaking, behold, a bright cloud overshadowed them; and behold a voice out of the cloud, saying, "This is My beloved Son, with whom I am well-pleased; listen to Him!" And when the disciples heard this, they fell on their faces and were much afraid. And Jesus came to them and touched them and said, "Arise, and do not be afraid." And lifting up their eyes, they saw no one, except Jesus Himself alone. And as they were coming down from the mountain, Jesus commanded them, saying, "Tell the vision to no one until the Son of Man has risen from the dead." And His disciples asked Him, saying, "Why then do the scribes say that Elijah must come first?" And He answered and said, "Elijah is coming and will restore all things; but I say to you, that Elijah already came, and they did not recognize him, but did to him whatever they wished. So also the Son of Man is going to suffer at their hands." Then the disciples understood that He had spoken to them about John the Baptist.

Matthew 17:1-13, NASB

Through the years we have encountered an oversupply of books and sermons—a few of the sermons mine—on the pains and problems of the church. We have debated and discussed at length over the decline in baptisms, the leveling off of Sunday School attendance, and the general apathy concerning the considerations of God.

We have criticized and defended those who "leave the ministry," and probably a certain number should—leave, that is. We are also faced with many ministers who wish they could leave and those who wish some others would. Yet, we must stop and reason together about the direction in which the church is going and ought to go.

Several years ago *The Alabama Baptist* carried a guest editorial from a Methodist, Dr. Robert Wilson, who observed: "Many pastors are leaving because of disillusionment with the church. As a group, ex-pastors and those considering leaving are highly pessimistic about the church as an effective institution. They feel they are leaving a dying institution."

Dr. Wilson continued: "By holding course, we run into plenty of heavy weather. But we have never believed that it's possible to change with every wind and reach any destination. Churches are being buffeted by gales which seem to come from every point of the compass. But we would think that they, of all institutions, should try to ride it out on the true heading established long ago, making only such corrections as seem essential to survival.

"The government is under attack; business and industry are. Our whole system of values is being tossed about. All will survive if captains keep their heads and do not give in to the panic. Perhaps churches think they are different—that theirs is a special case, that social change, controversy, and transitory disaffection by rising generations will surely wreck them.

"Some ministers obviously believe churches are 'dying institutions.' With all respect we suggest that they are too easily frightened, too thin-skinned, and too long insulated from the heat of the kitchen," Dr. Wilson concluded.

All the storms that do blow upon the church from without, and all those that swell from within, should cause us to check our compasses and perhaps reset our sails. But these storms should not cause us to flee in fear. We have the mountaintop experiences, but we cannot—and we should not—remain there. True, down from the mountaintop, amid the tempestuous storms, we sometimes cry, "Carest Thou not that we perish?" (see Matt. 8:25, KJV). But in those hours of disappointment, heartbreak, and uncertainty, we are actually looking in the wrong direction, as did the disciples out in the boat with Jesus.

When we remove our gaze from Jesus, as did Peter on another occasion (see Matt. 14:28*ff.*), we begin to sense that sinking feeling. When we start watching one another with envy and jealousy, we falter. When we become suspicious of one another, we bog down and fail to "run with patience the race which is set before us."

Along with this passage from Matthew 17, where the emphasis is on "Jesus only" (see KJV), we ought to read and reread Hebrews 12:1-3:

> Therefore, since we have so great a cloud of witnesses surrounding us, let us also lay aside every encumbrance, and the sin which so easily entangles us, and let us run with endurance the race that is set before us, fixing our eyes on Jesus, the author and perfecter of faith, who for the joy set before Him endured the cross, despising the shame, and has sat down at the right hand of the throne of God. For consider Him who has endured such hostility by sinners against Himself, so that you may not grow weary and lose heart.

In many sports the instruction is: "Keep your eye on the ball." In baseball, batting instructors sound redundant with, "Kid, keep your eye on the ball all the way through your swing." In golf it goes, "Keep your head down, and keep your eye on the ball." And we will never have assurance and poise in our ministry until we keep our eyes fixed and focused on the Lord Jesus Christ!

Chester E. Swor, an inspiration to Baptists and others for over four decades, reminds us:

> The individual must be anchored to God. This anchoring begins, of course, with personal faith in Jesus Christ, but it will not be adequate anchorage if the Christian has not laid deeper and deeper hold upon God. This deepening hold

will include a perpetually growing faith, an increasing possession of God's Word, a maturing prayer power, and a growing surrender of total self to the will of God. Many Christians do not bear up well in the crucible test—not because they are not anchored to God in faith, but because the initial anchoring which brought salvation has not been developed into mature consecration.[1]

There is exactly the key for the individual Christian and for the church as a body.

In our text, Peter, James, and John had drawn apart with their Lord into a high mountain. Many commentators think it was Mount Hermon near Caesarea Philippi. Wherever it was, there transpired one of the rarest experiences ever beheld by mortals. Under divine control, there occurred a remarkable exception to the normal course of our Lord's life and ministry.

Jesus was invested with outward glory. He was "transfigured before them," His face shining like the sun, perhaps reminding them of the account of Moses as he had descended from the mountain centuries before, when "the skin of his face shone." Jesus' garments were transformed into luminescent grandeur.

For a moment He laid aside His humble guise. His servant form became radiant with heavenly brightness.

Some think that John (1:14) refers to the experience he had had, along with Peter and James on the Mount of the Transfiguration. But John most certainly had in mind more than that brief period when a dazzling luster shone upon the form and face of the Master. John was thinking of Jesus' loving deeds, His beautiful teachings, His devotion to God and man, the glory of His wisdom, goodness, love, and power. The glory of the incarnate Word was not seen by all the world, for these were men on earth with whom He came in constant, almost daily, contact, who never really knew Him or perceived His glory. He was a light shining in the darkness, and yet was never thoroughly comprehended. But those who received Him beheld His glory, the moral glory of His being, the mysterious glory of His person, the divine glory in revelation as God's eternal wisdom.[2]

Moses and Elijah were recognized by the disciples, even as they talked with Jesus. And after the conversation was finished, Peter suggested that they ought to have a building program. They could erect three tabernacles. While Peter was preoccupied with His meager plans (and all plans outside of God's will are exactly that—meager), the cloud overshadowed them. Then the voice of God the Father was heard, declaring pleasure in His only begotten Son. "This is my beloved Son, with Whom I am well-pleased; listen to Him!" Does that sound familiar? At His baptism in Jordan, the Spirit of God descended like a dove and lit upon Jesus. "And lo a voice from heaven, saying, This is my beloved Son, in whom I am well pleased" (Matt. 3:17; see also v. 16, KJV).

As was often the case in the Word of God, Jesus' followers were awe-stricken and afraid. "They fell on their faces and were much afraid" (v. 6). Likewise, the children of Israel at the foot of Mount Sinai had begged Moses to request that God stop speaking. They were petrified at His might and power.

As He always does, Jesus desires to reassure His followers. "Jesus came to them and touched them and said, 'Arise, and do not be afraid.' And lifting up their eyes, they saw no one except Jesus Himself alone" (vv. 7-8).

Now, I do not care to spiritualize here. Neither do I want to sound overly "pious." I am often uneasy with people who strive so hard to be "good" and "pious." But I would call to your attention that the passage starts out with, "And six days later. . ." (v. 1). "Six days later." Six days after what?

Six days after the episode at Caesarea Philippi when Jesus asked His disciples the supreme question, "Who am I?" After they batted around the views of the populace, and a few of their own ideas, it was impetuous Peter who once again stepped to the forefront.

He was like the bright child who raises his hand trying to answer every question. He wanted to build not one, not two, but three tabernacles. He was the one who would never, never forsake his Lord. No sir. In the Garden of Gethsemane, he would pull out his sword and cut off the ear of the high priest's servant. He was the guy who tried to walk on the water to Jesus. Yes, Peter, Cephas, the Rock "left no stone unturned."

He brazenly declared—and he was precisely correct: "Thou art the Christ, the Son of the living God" (Matt. 16:16, KJV). Only a few verses later this same apostle was severely rebuked by his Lord. "Get behind me, Satan! You are a stumbling block to Me; for you are not setting your mind on God's interests, but man's" (Matt. 16:23). There's no doubt about it. Old Peter is bound to have been a Baptist, bless his heart!

On the basis and ground of Peter's confession, Jesus began to reveal to His disciples the ultimate nature of His work and kingdom. This He did by pointing out the path He would follow—the road to the cross, the route of sacrificing His life as a ransom for the sins of all mankind. Verse 21 of chapter 16 is revealing:

> From that time Jesus Christ began to show His disciples that He must go to Jerusalem, and suffer many things from the elders and the chief priests and scribes, and be killed, and be raised on the third day.

Verse 22 displays the stubbornness of Peter: "And Peter took Him aside and began to rebuke Him, saying, 'God forbid it, Lord! This shall never happen to you.'" That is when Jesus, to use an old Irish expression, "lowered the boom" on Peter, "Get behind Me, Satan!" Like us, Peter could be so right one moment and so wrong the next.

In verse 16 he had made his marvelous confession, but in verse 22 he had protested even the thought of Jesus' carrying out the Father's will in sacrificial death. Little did Peter know that if Jesus had not gone through with His death, He could not have carried out His atoning action—and He could not have followed through on His very Messiahship as the Son of the living God.

Six days later Jesus was transfigured, and Moses and Elijah appeared to converse with Him.

You may recall that after Jesus was tempted and tested in the wilderness at the beginning of His ministry, angels came and ministered to Him. "Then the devil left Him; and behold, angels came and began to minister to Him" (Matt. 4:11). Now, as Jesus faced His impending death on the cross, he was ministered to by Moses, representative of the Law, and Elijah, standing for the prophets.

How like us those disciples were! Sometimes dense. Wavering in faith. Stubborn like an Ozarks mule. Spiritually befuddled. They simply could not understand the significance of their Master. At first they followed Him as a teacher, but even they were always misunderstanding His teachings. And they could ask more stupid questions!

Finally they began sounding like parrots as they repeated the insistent question, "What manner of man is this?" At Caesarea Philippi, Jesus inquired to ascertain how far they had gone in comprehending Him. Most of them had ventured no farther than to place Him among the prophets of the Old Testament. Many professing Christians today must be kin to those short-sighted disciples.

Now was the time for them to know for sure, first of all, that He was the Messiah—and second, for them to recognize that the old must pass away. It would not do for them to pour His "new wine" into old, rotten wineskins. "They saw no one, except Jesus Himself alone."

Jesus only!

[Peter] was so caught up, so thrilled with this experience of inspiration that he wanted to stay on the mountaintop. He did not want to go back down to the valley where there was suffering, heartache, and misery. He did not want to go to Jerusalem where death awaited His Master. He wanted to remain there in isolation and in inspiration. . . . Peter loved this experience and wanted to prolong it as long as possible. He, in fact, was content to let the experience be an end in itself. He was willing to forget about the conflicts, crises, and the crucifixion which lay ahead. He thought, *Wouldn't it be better to remain on the mountain in heavenly fellowship?*[3]

The effect of the transfiguration, as I understand it, was to teach the apostles a deeper reverence for their Master, Who, under circumstances of outward humiliation, was really displaying grace and truth as God's beloved Son. Moses and Elijah discussed His exodus with Him. To the premier representatives of the Law and the Prophets, the departure of Jesus by the path of the cross, the resurrection, and the ascension was an anticipated, familiar truth, but they were not permitted to speak with the three apostles. All were there to pay homage to Him. The accrediting voice came from the "shekinah" cloud itself. Our hope, like that of the apostles, is in seeing "no one, except Jesus Himself alone."

Jesus only!

We must view Christ as the only hope and source of salvation and eternal life for a sin-cursed, hell-bound world. Before he died, J. Pierpont Morgan, often-misunderstood mogul and at one time the richest man on earth, testified:

I commit my soul into the hands of my Saviour, in full confidence that having redeemed it and washed it in His most precious blood, He will present it faultless before the throne of my Heavenly Father, and I intreat my children to maintain and defend at all hazard and at any cost of personal sacrifice, the blessed doctrine of the complete atonement for sin through the blood of Jesus Christ, once offered, and through that alone.

Not too long ago I learned a new word, "cavitation." Cavitation occurs when a high-speed propeller loses its bite on water, creating a partial vacuum, loss of thrust, and excessive shaft speed. Many churches and individuals are suffering from cavitation. They are spending an excessive amount of time and energy seeking to know "the times and seasons," or using a few words of Jesus in an effort to contradict other words of Jesus, so they can be excused from all-out witnessing and genuine effort. They have lost their bite on the water of reality, and have created a vacuum in which saccharin-sweet piety can thrive, while people's eyes are turned away from Jesus and are starving for the Bread of Life and thirsting for the Water of Life.

Many suffer from a lack of relevance and clout. They want to remain on the mountain without going down into the valley. They remind you of the story of the preacher who climbed up into the belfry of his church steeple in the hope of getting closer to God. He remained empty and unblessed, and finally heard a tiny, faraway voice calling Him. "Who is it?" the preacher asked, perplexed. Came the answer, "It's the Lord, my son, I am down here among My people."

Many sincere Christians spend hours talking about the "charismatic" movement—and we ought to desire "earnestly the best gifts" (1 Cor. 12:31*a*, KJV). But they are caught up in gifts to the detriment of going out into the highways and hedges with an effective Christian witness. They are like Peter who wanted to remain on top of the mountain and bask in the glory of Jesus' transfiguration. People talk about being a charismatic people when they need to be a "pneumatic" people. *Pneuma*, of course, is the Greek word for Spirit.

When we look out and see no one but Jesus, it is amazing how our priorities will change, how many seemingly important hobby horses will ride off into the sunset and into oblivion. If only we could catch the essence of Helen H. Lemmel's touching song:

> O soul, are you weary and
>   troubled?
> No light in the darkness you see?
> There's light for a look at the
>   Savior,
> And life more abundant and free!
> Turn your eyes upon Jesus,
> Look full in His wonderful face,
> And the things of earth will grow
>   strangely dim
> In the light of His glory and grace.[4]

When we listen to His Commission, "Ye shall be witnesses unto Me in Jerusalem, in Judea, in Samaria, and unto the uttermost parts of the world," how our emphases change!

I am persuaded that compassion and concern are desperately needed among Baptists—and every Christ-oriented group. This is not concern about programs, buildings, institutions, or denominational life. All of these are necessary, but they are intended as the means, but we so often make them ends in themselves. As Christians we can become locked into our own little circles or coteries, "our kind of folks." We are called on to witness wherever we are, to engage in "life-style" evangelism, to win souls in the workplace, at home, in the restaurant, in the service station, on the streets—everywhere. What was the summary statement about the early Christians? "They went everywhere preaching the Word."

Read Matthew 9 and let it haunt you. When Jesus saw the multitudes He was "moved with compassion upon them, because they fainted, and were scattered abroad, as sheep having no shepherd" (v. 36, KJV). We often sing "The Great Physician now is near, the sympathizing Jesus." He is our Model, and yet we continue on in our unconcern, our coldness, our callousness, catering to ourselves and letting the rest of the world go to hell.

Concern does not seem to be in our church programming. We do not have on our church calendars—or in our denominational calendars—"A Concern Commitment Day." Perhaps we should. Yet, we cannot work up concern. How does concern seize us? It does when we are willing to see no one except Jesus Christ Himself. Jesus only!

Concern comes when we are willing to view the world through the compassionate eyes of the Lord Jesus.

Concern comes when we visualize our children half-starved, half-naked, half-savage on the broad road which leads to destruction.

Concern comes when we hear, truly hear, Jesus challenging us, "As the Father has sent Me, I also send you" (John 20:21).

Concern comes when we respond to the command, "Ye shall be witnesses unto me" (Acts 1:8, KJV).

Our church in Amarillo, like many others, has sent out groups of laypersons on evangelistic crusades in cooperation with the Foreign Mission Board of our denomination. Our first overseas trip was to Japan and Korea in 1970. That group ranged in age from twelve to past seventy.

As they prepared for the effort, I heard them literally begging the Lord to let them see nothing but Jesus Christ and Him alone. They further prayed that they would have no mixed motives—that they would go for no other reason than to witness to the saving power of the Lord Jesus. They experienced amazing evangelistic victories for Christ, all but unbelievable except to those who were there.

On July 27, our people left Seoul by bus to be with Brother Johnny Yoo and his church for 2 PM services, at which time the church building would be dedicated and Johnny ordained to the gospel ministry. This church was so far away from the cities that Missionary Cloyce Starnes explained that the villagers had never before seen an American woman.

There were no roads for cars, let alone buses. Consequently we arrived at 6:10 that night, over four hours late.

But the people were still waiting and praying for us. Our service was awfully short because we had to return to Seoul before curfew. Later Brother Johnny Yoo wrote us, and I quote his exact words:

> First of all, allow me to tell you my appreciation to you right now. I could hardly find the words to express my sincere gratitude to you and your dear members who've been here on July 27 for our church dedication service and my ordain service. I could never forget that day through my whole life. You will never know what your trip meant to me. I have never been received such wonderful spiritual gift through that hour.
>
> Just let me share with you one thing of it today. Through your short sermon, Holy Spirit moved. Five young men (unbelievers) who came to church on that day to see Americans and have fun they said, and those five young men came to me at night and asked me a question. They said, "In the American pastor's sermon (that mean you) he said we must give everything to win those lost souls as we dedicate this church, and as we cooperate to save these lost souls. What is the meaning of those lost souls? Who he mean that lost soul?" they said. So I could have a chance to talk with them about salvation and how to be saved. They all made decisions, and two of them were baptized last week.

Everywhere we go we are to exalt, glorify, and magnify Jesus Christ because we know how to do nothing else. One's pet ideas and carnal concerns are of no consequence. When we focus on Jesus, the Holy Spirit moves in power and people are born into the Kingdom of God. Christ alone is the source of salvation.

All over our land are churches which have felt they could reach few, if any, for Christ. But a handful of members turned their eyes upon Jesus. People had pessimistically alibied, "Folks are gospel-hardened. They can't be reached." But a little band of believers fixed their eyes upon the Savior. One by one people began receiving Christ as Lord and Savior. Why? Because a handful of people began to take the Word of God seriously, began to center on Jesus, began to believe that "the gospel is the power of God unto salvation to everyone that believeth" (Rom. 1:16, KJV).

For victory we must see Jesus only.

Today there may be as many discouraged people in the churches as there are on the outside. Many are defeated in the pressures of life. They want to be right and to do right. Somehow they have failed, and they are being swept away into the valley of despair. They wonder if there is "Victory in Jesus."

We must help them recognize that there is victory in Him, that the "battle is the Lord's." Let someone else worry about the Dow-Jones averages, our foreign policy, and all kinds of peripheral issues. Peter declared, "Christ hath also suffered for us, leaving us an example, that we should follow his steps" (1 Pet. 2:21, KJV).

This is our business, walking in His steps. Looking to Him. Following Him. Witnessing for Him. Living for Him. Not to keep up with this hollow, abominable society. Therefore, let us turn again in our pulpits, our Sunday School classes, our women's organizations, our men's groups, our recreation programs, our music, and the entire ministry of the church . . . and point to Jesus as the source of victory, whether on the mountaintop or down in the valley, "valley so low."

Down in the valley, or upon the mountain steep,
Close beside my Saviour would my soul ever keep;
He will lead me safely in the path that He has trod,
Up to where they gather on the hills of God.

Follow! Follow! I would follow Jesus!
Anywhere, everywhere, I would follow on!
Follow, follow! I would follow Jesus!
Everywhere He leads me I would follow on!
—W. O. Cushing

7

Busy Here and There

And as thy servant was busy here and there, he was gone.
And the king of Israel said unto him, So shall thy judgment
be: thyself hast decided it.

1 Kings 20:40, KJV

For two successive years, Ben-hadad, king of Syria,
warred on Ahab and his kingdom, Israel. The first year
Ben-hadad arrived with his vast army including thirty-two
allied nations. But before the battle he had sent word to
Ahab, "Your silver and gold are mine, as are your prettiest
wives, and the best of your children" (1 Kings 20:3, TLB).

Ahab tremblingly sat down and envisioned the crack
troops of thirty-three nations coming against Israel, so he
sent back word: "You may have my silver and my gold, the
prettiest of my wives, and the best of my children." Then the
pitiful monarch discovered what many of us learn too late—
that when you are frightened and intimidated by a bully,
there are always more demands in the offing.

Ben-hadad then shot back this communication. "Not

only are your silver and gold mine, the prettiest of wives, the best of your children, but when I have taken those, my men will search your palace and the homes of your people, and my men will take away whatever they like" (see v. 6).

This was even more than measly Ahab could stand, so he called in his advisors. They counseled him, "Send word to Ben-hadad that enough is enough. You can go this far and no farther."

There is a point beyond which honor, even after being dragged in the dust, must respond, "No more. This is it. This is as far as you are going." Many a puny frightened kid has had to learn this lesson and decide, "If I am going to live past ten or eleven years old, I am going to have to start fighting back, even if it does kill me!"

The message was sent. "You may have only what you were originally promised, but no more." Came back the boast from Ben-hadad, "May the gods do more to thee than I am going to do to you, if I do not turn Samaria into handfuls of dust" (see v. 10).

In verse 11 was Ahab's answer. To couch it in modern language, the Hebrew idiom means something like, "Don't bank on it. Don't count your chickens before they hatch." When Ben-hadad received the message, the declaration from Israel that its people would no longer be insulted and trampled underfoot, Ben-hadad's troops moved with a vengeance.

The army of boastful Ben-hadad was slaughtered, and the Syrian king managed to escape on horseback to return with an even greater force the following year, led this time not by kings, but by generals.

Before that strategic battle, Ben-hadad gathered his aides together. He was advised, "Israel's God is a God of the hills—that is where His strength is—so fight the Israelites on the plains, and they will have no advantage over you from their God."

So the Syrians camped in the Valley of Aphek, and Israel, like herds of goats, on the barren heights. Then the prophet of God reported to Ahab. "The Syrians think that Jehovah is a hill God and not also the God of the valley. So Jehovah says to you, 'I will put this host in your power and let you see I am eternal'" (see 20:28).

Then the Israelites and the Syrians launched their second immense, blood-letting battle. The army of Israel killed 100,000 Syrians the first day! (see v. 29). The reference is to "footmen" slain, so many more Syrian horsemen and charioteers may have perished. The remainder of the Syrian army was routed to the town of Aphek and hid behind a wall. Yes sir, the wall fell on them and killed all 27,000 of them!

Ben-hadad's officers, who had escaped with him, began to think (which was dangerous for them!), sharing their ideas with him:

> Behold now, we have heard the kings of the house of Israel are merciful kings, please let us put sackcloth on our loins and ropes on our heads, and go out to the king of Israel; perhaps he will save your life (v. 31).

Can you imagine it? Suggesting that Ben-hadad live when he had offered no mercy to the Israelites when he thought the Syrians and their allies had the upper hand. Perhaps the Syrians surmised the Israelites were soft—maybe soft in the head, but they felt the effort was worth a try.

The battle was given to Ahab, certainly not because of him (the unscrupulous character), but because those Israelites were God's people.

There is almost a parallel here. Our nation was once considered the mightiest on earth. That had been true of Israel under Solomon. But in the world community today, other nations wonder about our power. Observers feel the Russians may have the military edge on us, even though they continue to offer extravagant "peace" terms to the extent of offering to do away with all nuclear devices.

The rest of the world does not necessarily think Americans are merciful—but that they are soft. And because we still claim to be a "Christian nation," they do whatever they will to our citizens and our flag. Because we have lived in affluence, seated in the lap of luxury—and want no war with any nation—it sometimes seems there are few principles for which Americans will fight.

We are sidetracked by the pursuit of pleasure. Drugs are of epidemic proportions. One reason we cannot stop drug traffic is because many law enforcement officers are in cahoots with the traffickers, and that comes to light nearly every day in the newspapers. And sometimes the courts are not helping. A recent newspaper article in a Southern city dealt with the fact that two big dope dealers were let off on a

$10,000 bond each, even though the prosecutor wanted to set their bonds at one million dollars each!

Corruption and graft are rampant in places high and low, so the rest of the world thinks it can thumb its noses at us. Our enemies believe they can chip away a bit at a time until we finally capitulate and crumble. Decades ago, Communist planners declared that the U.S. would sin and spend itself into oblivion.

So it was with those ancient peoples. Even though the Israelites were considered mighty in battle, they were also infused with the highest ethical and moral standards on earth—given to them by Almighty God, Who loves every nation.

Ben-hadad's flunkies approached Ahab, who was surprised that Ben-hadad was still alive. He asked, "Is he yet alive?" "Yes," came the answer. "He is my brother, go get him," answered Ahab (see vv. 32-33). Ahab invited Ben-hadad up into his chariot. The Syrian king vowed that he would restore the cities his father had taken from Ahab's father. He also promised that Israel could establish trading posts in Damascus, as his father had done in Samaria.

Then Ahab let Ben-hadad go free. Was that the charitable, merciful, right action? There was the man who in two successive years had waged war with God's people with the intent of plundering and pillaging Israel and carrying away the most beautiful women and the healthiest children into captivity. Of this cutthroat, murderous king, Ahab stated: "He is my brother."

Well I remember personally hearing the late R. G. Lee

preach at an evangelistic conference in Mobile, Alabama. He was taking to task those who preach "the Fatherhood of God and the brotherhood of man" without stressing that such cannot exist without saving faith in the Lord Jesus Christ. Lee, in his inimitable manner, asked, "You mean to tell me that Khrushchev is my brother? I disown the rascal!" And the "amens" rolled.

One unnamed prophet in the land of Israel realized that an unholy alliance was not the plan of God, so he disguised himself as a wounded soldier and waited beside the road for the king to come by. When the king appeared, the prophet announced, "Your servant went out into the midst of battle; and behold a man turned aside and brought a man to me and said, 'Guard this man; for if for any reason he is missing, then your life shall be for his life, or else you shall pay a talent [probably equivalent to $2000] of silver. And while your servant was busy here and there, he [the guarded man] was gone.' And the king of Israel said to him, 'So shall your judgment be; you yourself have decided it'" (1 Kings 20:39-40).

In other words, "You will have to pay," commanded the king. Then the prophet revealed his true identity and said, "Thus says the Lord, Because you have let go out of your hand the man whom I had devoted to destruction, therefore your life shall go for his life, and your people for his people" (v. 42).

Now, virtually every commentary I have read goes to great lengths to explain how, in our day, we should not relate to such a gory, bloody chapter as this; how we must understand that people of that barbaric day understood little of the milk of human kindness. I do not agree with this namby-pamby idea of trying to explain away passages we do not find appealing and appetizing. I recognize that sounds horrible to some supersensitive ears, for we have been conditioned that we ought to be solicitous to everyone.

There is a time for being firm. Most of our churches today seem to accept whatever they please. In many areas, standards are almost non-existent. That is why many churches are losing out, when they ought to be winning against the forces of the devil and unrighteousness.

Yes, we are supposed to love every man, woman, and child on the face of this earth. At the same time God has never asked up to be wimps in dealing with the devil and his followers.

We often think we can sit back and do nothing—and that all will be well. When will we begin to believe the often-quoted statement of Edmund Burke, "All that is necessary for the triumph of evil is that good men do nothing"? The devil walks to and fro as a roaring lion, seeking those whom he would devour. We wrestle not against flesh and blood but against principalities, against powers, against rulers of spiritual wickedness in high places. We are in a battle for survival, and we Christians act as though we are going to a pink tea.

The forces of wickedness will steal all they can—our life, our liberty, our pursuit of happiness. They will endeavor to grab our liberty to proclaim the glorious Gospel of God. Right now there are places in the world where preaching the

Gospel of Christ is punishable by death. There are times when we must stand and stand firm, when we must fight to protect that which God has given to us. That time already may have arrived for us, as it did for Israel in our text.

Prior to the Second World War, France, already known worldwide for its bon vivant life-style, had lost its will to fight. After all, the Maginot Line would protect France from the Germans—it was impregnable.

Through partying and immorality, the attentions of the people were turned away from righteousness, and even the Catholic churches were deserted. France fell in a matter of days. Reports were that many French soldiers, instead of defending their country, were drinking in bistros and spending their money in brothels as the Nazis marched into Paris. How close are we to that deplorable condition?

Yes, many believers become upset when they treat a passage like this, alibiing, "I don't understand how you can be a Christian, read this, and say that it has to be taken literally!" God is sovereign, and He is under no obligation to give us explanations for His commands or His will!

But if you study the Scriptures, and history outside of the Scriptures, you can plainly see that God's primary purpose has always been the salvation of lost mankind, the proclamation of the Good News of eternal life, and anybody or anything that stands in the way and will not repent, God will move—in order that the multitudes of the earth may at least have the privilege of hearing the message of redemption. The Syrians of our text and the Amalekites in the era of Samuel—and numerous other peoples—have been impediments to the message of Almighty God. In addition to that, do not forget that God has always protected His people. Yes, multitudes of His people have perished, but God has always preserved His remnant.

Now note how this chapter closes out. "So the king of Israel went to his house sullen and vexed, and came to Samaria" (v. 43).

There was no repentance from his lack of backbone, no remorse because of his failure to be obedient to God, no sorrow because of his league with an enemy who was bent on the destruction of God's messengers. He just went home angry and sullen. There was no pain because his people were going to perish because of his lack of moral fiber and spiritual leadership.

Then follows chapter 21, where a weak and spoiled King Ahab pouts and weeps because he covets, and cannot have, the vineyard of Naboth, which was located close to the palace. As you recall, the most famous sermon of R. G. Lee was "Payday Someday" concerning Ahab's perfidy in seizing Naboth's vineyard and having poor Naboth put to death. Naboth did no harm; he was only the keeper of a vineyard passed down to him from generation to generation. Yet, Ahab let Ben-hadad, the enemy of God's people, loose but executed Naboth, a mild-mannered grower of grapes. What an irony and what a travesty of justice!

My dear readers, if anyone under heaven ought to understand the principles of freedom and self-determination, Christians should, particularly here in the "land of the free and the home of the brave." We need to have a sense of justifiable joy about who we are, and about what this nation has accomplished under God. We Christians should lead out in love for our country.

Look about at your children, your grandchildren, your neighbors' children and granchildren. Surely we want them to have the same opportunities which were granted to our generation.

In a violent world like ours, where atheistic Communism is dead serious about burying us, where fanatics like Khadafy and Khomeini can terrorize thousands, where hateful dictators can reign in bloody terror and defy the free world, you are bound to realize that the hour has arrived for us to prayerfully, but urgently, prod our nation's leaders to make necessary decisions and take steps in keeping with the honor of this land.

Call me radical if you wish, but I believe it would be far better to die for our nation than to live in constant fear. Think back over the last several years—the imprisonment of fifty-four American hostages in Iran, the "suicide" bomb killing of almost 250 Marines in Beirut, Lebanon, the holding of hostages by various terrorist groups. And you recite a litany of devilish hate. If it can happen to them—to anybody, anywhere, anytime—it could happen here.

If there is a place from which the Gospel is to be preached, it is from this land. And if we lose the opportunity to share that message because we have thrown away the respect of the world, what will happen to our missionaries and others whom we have sent?

Let the late author Pearl Buck stir us:

The early missionaries were born warriors. To them religion was a banner under which to fight. No weak or timid soul could sail the seas to foreign lands and defy dangers and death unless he carried his religion as a banner under which even death would be a glorious end. . . . To go forth, to cry out, to warn, to save others—these were frightful urgencies of the soul already saved.[1]

There is a principle here, personal in application. It is this: each one of us is individually responsible—and then, as the body of Christ, collectively responsible. And we must decide what constitutes our major emphasis.

If our number-one priority is to be an affluent nation, to sit in self-petting and preening, we are doomed. If our number-one priority is to balance the Federal budget (a seemingly impossible feat), we have missed the mark. If our number-one priority is to pattern ourselves after the TV and movie stars, and "The Lifestyles of the Rich and Famous," hang black crepe on our doorknobs and yell out, "Stop the world. I want to get off!"

In relation to those who hate our country and commit attacks of terrorism, I am not suggesting that we always retaliate. There are no easy answers. We should pray for our President and the Congress as they grapple with our nation's course of action. Remember Ben-hadad. The more Ahab yielded to him, the more the Syrian king greedily demanded and wanted. But also remember that God Almighty, the Lord of hosts, intervened.

My prayer is that we will learn from 1 Kings 20 that we are called on to take a stand, to be firm, to sound off. Once we decide on our primary priority, we must be true to that chief duty, whatever lesser motives and considerations may tempt us to turn aside. Hear that unnamed prophet: "And as thy servant was busy here and there, he was gone." He was speaking a parable to Ahab. "Your responsibility, O king, was to win the battle, not for yourself, but for the glory and honor of Jehovah God; and while you were busy tending to the diplomatic language, he was gone. Ben-hadad was gone. While you were trying to make friends with an hater of Jehovah God, he was gone." An unholy alliance was formed.

Perhaps the prevalent cause of failure and frustration in many churches is exactly this: while we are busy here and there, the number-one responsibility goes undone. The chief work goes begging. And you know what that is—the winning of every possible soul to Jesus Christ. In our text the soldier's duty was to guard the important prisioner entrusted to him in the midst of battle. He accepted that either on the pain of death or a tremendous fine. He was charged to differentiate between the important and the unimportant, and to faithfully perform his assignment.

But he became "busy here and there." Soon the prisoner was gone. Surely this shouts out to all of us: "Be careful, individually and collectively, not to let the trivial steal from us the significant." "Seek ye first the kingdom of God, and his righteousness, and all these things shall be added unto you" (Matt. 6:33, KJV). "Go out into the highways and along the hedges, and compel them to come in, that my house may be filled" (Luke 14:23).

The crises of the last several years, even the untimely death of six U.S. astronauts in the space shuttle, have called us to our knees. These have summoned forth qualities of character which, a few years ago, seemed almost nonexistent. Amid unparalleled moral decay and sinful filth, there is an awakening to the strengths which lie dormant within our country. I have discovered, as you have, that young and old alike will come to the defense of this nation and her citizens. It is my solemn prayer that we will stand tall for whatever actions necessary for the honor of this land.

Here I issue a warning. We must not busy ourselves here and there with nonessentials at the cost of the essential. If you often sit at a desk as I do, you understand the futility of being sidetracked. Facing me is a mound of work, but I have trouble starting. So I decide to clean up my messy desk. Then I begin to shuffle papers until I can no longer shuffle them. But I am still not in a mood to work.

Then I begin to count paper clips and check the stapler. I must make sure there are paper clips aplenty, lest I have to search for them during the day. I have not used the stapler in months, but who knows? I may need it. Then I sharpen pencils. I have not used a pencil in years, but one never knows when I will use a pencil instead of my pen. Through all of this preparation, I am doing nit-picking jobs that will keep me from the main tasks. It happens to nearly all of us. And we must become better disciplined that we may be effective in the heavier demands made on us.

My denomination spends untold man and woman hours going through the paces of learning to reach people for

Christ, to win souls. We preach about it. We read books about it. We send out literature about it. No demonination on earth has better resources for soul-winning. We have "study courses," evangelism clinics and conferences, retreats, and every kind of rally. Yet, we baptized less people last year than we have in several years. We are busy here and there in preparation and study but doing practically nothing about winning people heart to heart and face to face.

High school and college students run into this dilemma. On Friday afternoon it is announced that you will face a crucial test on Monday morning. There is no ball game on the weekend, so you ought to have ample time to bone up for the test. But before you settle down to study, you must call several of your friends before your parents or college roommates have to use the phone. Then you decide that a snack will help, so you pop corn—or you grab an apple or a candy bar or a bowl of cereal. Then you discover that a must-see TV program is coming on. Either you wait until late Sunday night to study or study none at all. And you may fail the exam. "Busy here and there."

There is an old expression: "We don't set Rome afire. We merely fiddle while it burns!" We fiddle while the world plunges toward hell.

Being "busy here and there" spills over into every part of our lives. One reason for the drastic divorce rate is that husbands, wives, and children are so busy here and there, instead of building lasting, loving relationships. Many families are never all together, even when the children are small. Dad has his work, his clubs, his sports—hopefully no extramarital affairs. Mom has her housework (or she works outside the home), her activities, her aerobics class, her taxi service for the children, her part-time job selling cosmetics. By the time the children have reached nine years old, they are caught up in school projects, selling cookies and candy for the school, playing on the ball teams, going to music lessons, and collecting junk. Untold families are strangers within four walls.

This happens to friendships. We take our friends for granted, thinking, *They'll be there when I need them. They know I care.* But we seldom show that caring, so friendships erode. A "loving phone call" or a card dashed off quickly could make the difference. We are so busy stacking pieces of paper and arranging our trivia that we no longer have time for family and friends.

And this can happen at church. We become so "busy here and there." Countless members become so busy here and there that they start dropping out. Prayer meeting always seems to fall by the wayside first. Then there is the demise of the evening service for them. By and by they are not there at all, not necessarily because they are bad or totally unconcerned people but too busy with the wrong concerns. They began not to seek the kingdom of God and its righteousness.

All of the situations I have mentioned are tragedies. But one day we will not be too busy to die. We will not be too busy to stand before God, at the judgment seat of Christ for the saved and at the "great white throne of judgment" for the lost. "So then every one of us will give account of himself to God" (Rom. 14:12). Jesus Christ Himself will ask us to present a report of our stewardship. Does that make you the least bit nervous?

Will you let the convicting words of the Lord Jesus sink into your soul?

For what will a man be profited, if he gains the whole world and forfeits his soul? Or what will a man give in exchange for his soul? (Matthew 16:26).

The worst disaster is for one to lose or forfeit his own soul. Many have been so busy they have seemingly had no time for a relationship with the Lord Jesus. Others, who have trusted the Lord, have been so busy with the paper clips of life they have virtually bypassed the eternal verities. They have not realized we have but one life to live and to invest. Surely that life ought to be spent to best advantage for the maturing of the spirit, for the glory of God, and for the service of a lost and destitute world. "Only one life, 'Twill soon be past. Only what's done for Christ will last."

The late Dr. E. P. Alldredge preached a sermon on "The Question of Profit and Loss," the text being based on Matthew 16:24-28. This first point was: "If One Seeks and Gains the Whole World What Has He?" Of course, his question was only theoretical. Alldredge continued:

My friend, Dr. J. M. Carroll of Texas, set this out in seven points as follows: a. He could use only a small part of it. b. He could use that small part only for a little while. c. He could have no associates, no fellowship, and no comradeship. d. He could never have a real friend, or companion, or partner. e. He would have responsibilities and obligations which no human mind could understand and no human power fulfill. f. No part of his possessions, or all of them together, could take away his sins and give him peace with God. g. When he came to die, he could not carry any part of his riches or any one of his achievements with him.[2]

Are you so "busy here and there" that genuine life has passed you by?

8

Earnestly Contend for the Faith

Jude, the servant of Jesus Christ, and brother of James, to
them that are sanctified by God the Father, and preserved
in Jesus Christ, and called: Mercy unto you, and peace,
and love be multiplied. Beloved, when I gave all diligence
to write unto you of the common salvation, it was needful
for me to write unto you, and exhort you that ye should
earnestly contend for the faith which was once delivered
unto the saints.

Jude 1-3, KJV

Mrs. Orville Wilkinson, one of the dear members of our
church, vividly remembered that on the first Sunday that
First Baptist Church of Amarillo met in its new sanctuary,
Dr. Kyle Yates preached from this text. Since I learned of
that, I have wondered what was in his mind.

Moving to a new church plant and place of worship is usually cause for tremendous rejoicing. How Israel must have
celebrated when they entered the Temple built under the
leadership of Solomon!

At the same time I mused about Dr. Yates's message, I

remembered that Jude's Epistle was intended primarily to deal with unregenerate church members. I surely did wonder why Yates chose this text from the hundreds—yea, thousands—of texts he might have selected. Then I remembered that Jude's message was also one of priority.

Jude's message of priority concerned exposing unregenerate, unborn-again "church members," and warning against false teachers and self-serving leaders.

A pastor is thrilled when he has the blessed privilege of delivering a message of good tidings. We all like pleasant news, but there are times when a word must come through, regardless of the circumstances—even if that message is one of gloom and doom.

President Woodrow Wilson loved peace. He was the father of the League of Nations, yet his own Senate refused to ratify the treaty which would have given the U.S. membership. Their rejection of the League was one reason Wilson fell into a deep depression. Many think his disappointment and remorse finally led to his untimely death.

How well Wilson must have recalled the dreadful evening in April of 1917 when our nation had declared war on the Axis powers. Wilson desired freedom and peace for this nation, but war loomed on the horizon. President Wilson did not want to discuss it, or even to think about it. Yet, the unpleasant duty remained. On that April evening, with rain pelting the nation's capital, Wilson stood before Congress to read his message:

> It is a dreadful thing to lead this great people into the war, into the most terrible and disastrous of all wars, civiliza-

tion seeming to be in the balance. But right is more precious than peace . . . and we shall fight for the things which we have always carried nearest our hearts. . . . To such a task we can dedicate our lives and our fortunes, everything we are and everything we have.

Wilson was a statesman of peace who made a declaration of war in an emergency situation of priority.

Jude delivered such a pronouncement. He immediately explained that he had wanted to write a letter of peace, of joy, and of the blessings arising out of our common salvation in Christ Jesus. But he found himself instead thrust into the unpleasant task of dealing with heresy, with apathy, with people who wanted to serve themselves rather than others. Thus, he wrote a fervent appeal for the brethren to "earnestly contend for the faith."

At times we all experience Jude's pain. How many military personnel like to deliver the personal message: "Your husband has been killed in the line of duty"? Only an unstable person yearns to dwell on constant negativism. Most of us like "sweetness and light," as Matthew Arnold called it. We do not enjoy the roar of artillery, the taste of blood, but there comes a time when we must leave our towers of tranquility to grapple with the insects gnawing at the foundation.

What was the malicious force, the evil that literally thrust Jude out of the tower and pushed him into the clash? The Gnostics were abounding in the churches, those who claimed they were in possession of the true "gnosis" or knowledge. They called themselves the intellectual "in" crowd. They claimed to have intellectual and spiritual superiority over ordinary people, because they allegedly involved themselves in the "deeper mysteries."

Cults and schisms, at least spiritually akin to Gnostics, abound and thrive today. All of them contend that they alone have the secrets to life here and the hereafter. Many of them quote the Bible but use it for their own weird doctrines. The majority of these modern-day Gnostics are built around a personality, usually a dynamic individual who makes all kinds of promises of health, wealth, and special benefits. Sadly, throngs of empty persons rush to these false messiahs and their brand of religion.

Gnosticism, as you may remember, considered all material or physical things as either unreal or inherently evil. And if all physical things were evil, then God of course could not enter a human body, as did Jesus, the incarnate Son of God. None of the Gnostics believed that Jesus Christ was incarnate in human flesh. Jude and John believed that it was just as evil to reject the humanity of Jesus as it was not to believe in His Deity, because Jesus is the God-man. "The Word became flesh" (see John 1:14). Listen to John in these passages:

> Beloved, believe not every spirit, but try the spirits whether they are of God: because many false prophets are gone out into the world. Hereby know ye the Spirit of God: Every spirit that confesseth that Jesus Christ is come in the flesh is of God: And every spirit that confesseth not that Jesus Christ is come in the flesh is not of God: and this is the spirit of antichrist, whereof ye have heard that it should

come; and even now is already in the world (1 John 4:1-3, KJV).

Whosoever shall confess that Jesus is the Son of God, God dwelleth in him, and he in God (1 John 4:15, KJV).

Whosoever believeth that Jesus is the Christ is born of God: and every one that loveth him that begat loveth him also that is begotten of him. . . . Who is he that overcometh the world, but he that believeth that Jesus is the Son of God? (1 John 5:1,5, KJV).

For many deceivers are entered into the world, who confess not that Jesus Christ is come in the flesh. This is a deceiver and antichrist. . . . Whosoever transgresseth, and abideth not in the doctrine of Christ, hath not God. He that abideth in the doctrine of Christ, he hath both the Father and the Son. If there come any unto you, and bring not this doctrine, receive him not into your house, neither bid him God speed: For he that biddeth him God speed is partaker of his evil deeds (2 John 7-9, KJV).

Today we have the same kinds of enemies in new uniforms and going by different names. New theologies have arisen. Discarding the vocabulary and validity of the New Testament, these have also produced new kinds of church members, some who are self-appointed pathologists, qualified to perform his/her own autopsy on the church, and sometimes within the very church for which Christ died.

Jude had only one claim to authority by which he spoke. He was "the servant of Jesus Christ." What better credentials are there? This means more than an observer or a critic or a "hanger on." He was a disciple of Christ, and that means more than being concerned or curious. He was committed!

We are to "earnestly contend for the faith." Here "the faith" speaks of the body of truth taught in the Scriptures. For example, Acts 6:7, "A great company of the priests were obedient to the faith." Then, we read in Acts 16:5, "So the churches were strengthened in the faith." Felix and Drusilla, his wife, heard Paul speak "concerning the faith in Christ Jesus" (Acts 24:24, KJV). Paul admonished the deacons to hold "the mystery of the faith in a pure conscience" (1 Tim. 3:9). Paul spoke to Titus about "gainsayers" and added "for which cause reprove them sharply that they may be sound in the faith" (Titus 1:13).

In other words, what we are to believe, what we are to be, and what we are to do, according to the Scriptures, is bound up in "the faith that was once delivered unto the saints." Jude declared that we should earnestly contend for that faith. The Greek word is from a root meaning to "epiagonize," to suffer severely. The world is not the friend of truth. The case is exactly the opposite. Maybe you have heard the saying, "Truth is mighty, and it will prevail," but that is false. If the world were perfect, the statement would be true, but this is a world of sin and untruth. Truth, without our proclaiming it, will not of itself prevail.

There is a proverb in many languages which goes, "A lie will get halfway around the world, while truth is putting on its boots." Did anyone ever tell a lie on you? Did the correction ever overtake the lie? Not in a million years! One rotten apple in a barrel will rot the unblemished ones, but one good

apple will not make a barrel of rotten ones sound. One dis-
eased person can spread contagion throughout a city, but
one healthy person cannot impart soundness and wholeness
to the sick in a hospital. In this world, it is disease, not
health, that is contagious.

If you remember nothing else, let this dominate you.
Truth is mighty only when it has prophets and apostles who
are ready to do, to dare, and to die in its behalf. The Gospel
will not preach itself. We are commanded to go preach that
life-giving message. No good cause will automatically take
care of itself. "Eternal vigilance is the price of liberty," and
it is also the price of everything else worth having.

Ideas are the rulers of the world. I long ago heard the expression, "Load a gun with a bullet, and you can kill a ty-
rant. But load it with an idea, and you can kill tyranny."
Tremendous ruin has been wrought by wrong ideas, false-
hoods, untruths, and unbiblical doctrines.

"Contend earnestly"—scholars indicate that this Greek
word is the strongest in any language to express intensity of
struggle.

The Word of God declares that we are to "agonize," to
enter in at the "strait gate," for our salvation. But we are to
"epi-agonize" for the body of the faith. In other words,
whether or not we understand it, *the faith* is more important
than one's personal salvation, for the salvation of mankind
depends on *the faith*.

Gamaliel the Pharisee once made a statement before the
Sanhedrin and the apostles who were hailed before them. I
believe this man's opinion has been quoted to the detriment

of thousands down through the centuries. (See Acts 5:34-
39.) His speech sounds so good, so wise, and so clever on
the surface. Gamaliel was fair in warning the Sanhedrin
about their actions against the apostles but not too wise in
vv. 38-39:

> And now I say unto you, Refrain from these men, and let
> them alone: for if this counsel or this work be of men, it
> will come to nought: But if it be of God, ye cannot over-
> throw it; lest haply ye be found to even fight against God.

Now, that is quoted as the Law and the Gospel, but Gamaliel's statement is not the truth. Remember that even the
devil is quoted in God's Word, and he is a liar and twists the
truth. He started out by lying to our first parents, Adam and
Eve, "Ye shall not surely die." He lied, and the Scriptures
are responsible for quoting him accurately.

A farmer does not suggest, "Leave the weeds in my field
alone. If they be of man, they will come to nought, but if
they be from God I cannot destroy them, lest I be found
fighting against God."

A man has cancer. He normally does not answer, "Leave
it alone, for if it is of man, it won't harm me; if it is from
God I must not check it lest I be found fighting against
God."

Such abysmal nonsense is tolerated only in matters of
highest importance—in religious life. What of Buddhism,
Hinduism, the Muslim religion? They are still here after all
of these centuries, and yet they are false religions of the
world. There is only one way to God, the true and living

God, and that is the Lord Jesus Christ, the King of kings and Lord of lords.

The fiery Saul of Tarsus "epi-agonized" for his faith, meeting the Lord on the Damascus Road. There is no hope for the Gamaliels of the world, I am afraid. One Paul or one Jude is worth an acre of Gamaliels.

Today we are advised to be broad, and the narrow person is denounced, as well as pitied. Beloved, there are three respects in which was can be broad or narrow. In two of them we ought to be broad, and in one we dare not be anything but narrow.

We need to be broad in our sympathies. God loves the whole world. We must love the whole world, too, and no person's national origin or color or anything should hinder our love and our sympathy going out to every kindred and every tribe.

We ought to be broad in our horizons. The conclusions we reach must not be the results of ignorance or prejudice. We must be able to look beyond our prejudices to see the world as God saw it, so we can be moved, as Jesus was moved with compassion, by what we see.

But in our beliefs we should be narrow, for truth is narrow. Two plus two equals four—exactly that, no more, no less. There are thousands of numbers 2 + 2 do not make (error is broad). There is only one sum they do make (truth is narrow).

Scientific truth is narrow. Under ordinary circumstances at sea level, water freezes at 32 degrees Fahrenheit, precisely that, no more, no less. There are thousands of temperatures at which water does not freeze. But here comes a man who claims he is broader than that. He contends that water freezes at 20 degrees, 30 degrees, 65 degrees or any other number. "Just so long as he is sincere, it does not matter what temperature he chooses." Such folly is not accepted in the scientific field.

Historical truth is narrow. A given event took place in one particular way at one particular time. There are a thousand places and a thousand ways it did not occur, because historical truth is narrow.

Geographical truth is narrow. There is one right direction from where you are to Timbuktu, Bangor, Maine; Ypsilanti, Michigan. There are thousands of wrong directions. "Wrong-Way" Corrigan found that out when he ended up in Ireland instead of the West Coast. Poor Roy Riegels found out when he almost made a touchdown for the opposing team in the Rose Bowl.

Yet, I also want to remind you that many narrow people are still wrong. It is equally narrow to argue that $2 + 2 = 5$, and stick by it, as it is to state they equal 4. You can be narrow and be wrong. But if we are broad about truth, we are bound to be wrong. There is a certain religion which teaches that all religions are essentially the same. A good question to ask is: why was it necessary to found their religion, then?

With the eternal truths of God's Word we are to be narrow, but in the words of the apostle Paul, we are to go about "speaking the truth in love" (Eph. 4:15).

We are oftimes deterred from contending earnestly for the faith for fear that we will give offense. Most of us want to be winsome witnesses. We do not want to offend anyone about anything. Most of us want to get along and be happy with everybody and have them happy with us.

Surely we are opposed to cancer, tuberculosis, multiple sclerosis, muscular dystrophy—yes, and AIDS and herpes and venereal diseases of all types. We should be opposed to these because they do harm to people for whom Christ died.

If by being narrow in contending earnestly for the faith, we make enemies, at least we are in good company. Paul made enemies wherever he went. I doubt if Lystra would have voted him "Man of the Year." Fact is, they stoned him and left him for dead outside the city gates. He never would have made it for "Most Likely to Succeed" or "Wittiest." His enemies often beat him, stoned him, cursed him—and finally chopped off his head in Rome.

And our own living Lord made enemies so bitter and violent and vitriolic that they hounded Him to death, then crucified Him, and stood to laugh and jeer and boo while He died in agony.

Jude refers to the faith as "once delivered unto the saints." It was not invented by the cunning of mankind. That body of faith, embracing the basic tenets—the fundamentals—of the Word of God is not subject to change. It is incapable of improvement. Let methods change, let customs change, let fashions change. Whatever we can change to facilitate our sending the gospel, let us change. But let it everlastingly be written that we "epi-agonized for the faith."

For His own providential reasons, God has chosen us as

His vessels for carrying out the message of "the faith which was once delivered unto the saints." That faith must be preached and proclaimed because all the hopes of mankind center here. Without this faith the world would be enshrouded in a starless night!

9

Who's in the Dark?

Now as to the times and the epochs, brethren, you have no need of anything to be written to you.

For your yourselves know full well that the day of the Lord will come just like a thief in the night. While they are saying, "Peace and safety!" then destruction will come upon them suddenly like birth pangs upon a woman with child; and they shall not escape.

But you, brethren, are not in darkness, that the day should overtake you like a thief;

For you are all sons of light and sons of day. We are not of night nor of darkness.

So then let us not sleep as others do, but let us be alert and sober. For those who sleep do their sleeping at night, and those who get drunk get drunk at night.

But since we are of the day, let us be sober, having put on the breastplate of faith and love, and a helmet the hope of salvation.

For God has not destined us for wrath, but for obtaining salvation through our Lord Jesus Christ,

147

Who died for us, that whether we are awake or asleep, we may live together with Him.

Therefore encourage one another, and build up one another, just as you also are doing.
1 Thessalonians 5:1-11, NASB

With this passage, let me suggest you also read 2 Thessalonians 1:6-12 and 2:1-12.

More and more believers are coming around to the premillennial position of our Lord's Second Coming. I do not believe in condemning a person because he does not subscribe to this view, nor do I subscribe to making one's view of eschatology a test of faith or fellowship. But this doctrine is dear to my heart.

In 1 Thessalonians 4:13-18 is a clear picture of the rapture, the Lord's snatching away of His followers prior to the tribulation period. In that passage of Scripture the saints of God, every born-again believer, will rise to meet the Lord in the air. Then I affirm that they will return with Him in His victorious reign on earth, the millennium. If you do not agree with me, may the Lord still bless you!

The coming of Jesus will be, I believe, in two phases. First, He comes *for* His church, and then He comes *with* His church. So far as I can discover in the Word of God, there is no word which would indicate that there is to be such an event as a partial rapture when Jesus comes. That is, when He comes, some people claim He will receive the consecrated Christians, but He will leave behind the less-dedicated believers, those who have backslidden and grown cold. To me there is no biblical justification for that hodge podge.

If this were true, if the rapture were dependent on whether I had ever been a backslider, or whether I was a backslider shortly before the return of the Lord, then the rapture would be dependent upon my works as a Christian. Rather, the Scriptures clearly indicate that the prerequisite is being born again. And by backsliding I mean the cooling of fellowship between a believer and his Lord. I am not implying that a person can lose his salvation. No way. If a person is genuinely born again, he will always be born again, because he is kept by the power of God, not his own striving and working.

That raises a question: Is there no difference between the deep Christian who seeks day by day to live a holy life, and that slipshod Christian who is indifferent to living out and out for his Master? Yes, there is a tremendous difference, but this has to do with the question of rewards (see 1 Cor. 3:13-15). Some shall "be saved as by fire," but they shall be saved none the less. All believers will be caught up to meet the Lord in the air (see 1 Thess. 4:17). Many Christians will lose their reward *but not their salvation*. A reward is what you receive for your works as a Christian. Salvation is the free gift of God's grace, and we cannot and do not work to be saved. "For by grace are ye saved through faith, and that not of yourselves: it is the gift of God. Not of works lest any man should boast" (Eph. 2:8-9, KJV).

When the Lord Jesus Christ comes back to remove His own, it will mean an horrendous time for those left behind.

After the Lord comes and carries away those who are still living on earth, transforms their bodies, translates them, and they are caught with those who have died before, and they all meet the Lord in the air—it means for those left on earth a terrible time of stress, an awful period of perplexity. Pestilences and persecution and wars unimagined in the history of civilization. I believe this period of time, the tribulation, is to be seven years.

Whatever the length of time between the coming of the Lord to claim His own and His coming back with His own, that period is described in the Scriptures. It is referred to as a time of "great tribulation," "the time of Jacob's trouble," "the day of the vengeance of our God." It is referred to as "the day of the Lord." Whatever you call it, it will be the darkest period in the history of the world. The Roman sieges of Jerusalem will be nothing compared to the tribulation. The campaigns of Napoleon and Alexander the Great and the Caesars will seem like child's play. The holocaust will appear mild, the holocaust in which six million Jews were annihilated in the ovens and torture chambers of Belsen, Buchenwald, Ravenhorst, and those heinous death camps across Europe.

Do we have it straight in our minds that the Lord is coming back *for* His own? After the tribulation He will come back *with* His own. And when He comes back with His own, it will be for the purpose of establishing the millennial kingdom, the capital of which will be the city of Jerusalem. His coming back to establish His kingdom will commence the earth's Golden Age.

The Bible declares that we ought to rejoice over the prospect, if we have Jesus Christ as our Lord and Savior. Yet, what a horrific time that will be for the unsaved. Read the 24th chapter of Matthew concerning our Savior's predictions about those events. Now, I recognize that many believe the Olivet Discourse has nothing to do with the end times. But you have to balance spiritual upon spiritual and Scripture upon Scripture. Paul, in 1 and 2 Thessalonians, makes three references to these blood-curdling times.

In 1 Thessalonians 5:1-11 he tells us again, as he did in chapter 4, about the coming of Christ to claim His own, His coming for the saints. Then in 2 Thessalonians 1:6-12 he speaks about the second phase when He comes with his saints. In 2 Thessalonians 2:1-12, he writes about the awful events that will occur in between these two comings, the rapture and the apocalypse of Revelation 19:11-19.

The Lord will come for His own and meet them in the air—all believers. Seven years later He will come back with His own to reign for a thousand years. Paul shows that in between those two comings some severe happenings are to occur prior to the second resurrection and the banishment of Satan.

First of all, the Lord's coming for His own has a meaning both for the saved and the unsaved. What does it mean for the unsaved? Look at 1 Thessalonians 5:2: "For you yourselves know full well that the day of the Lord will come just like a thief in the night." A thief does not call ahead and announce, "I am going to rob your house. May I set up an appointment?" Our Lord has promised again and again that

He is coming, but He has not given us the date. And when he was here, He Himself did not know. But when He comes, it will be suddenly and unexpectedly (by the majority of the earth's population). We as Christians are expecting Him— we are to look for Him—but we simply do not know when.

Space will not permit me to dwell on the consternation which will sweep the earth. Millions will be missing. Panic will rage across the world like has never been experienced.

My friends, the lost of our day pay absolutely no attention to this doctrine. The fact is, many Christians are blasé about it. Many of them seem to feel that there will be no Second Coming, or either they are not at all concerned about it. Many non-Christians scoff. "Why, that's the most ridiculous thing I've ever heard of!" Let them sneer.

Jesus is coming back. I would like it if you would agree with my view, which I have agonized over for years. To me it is the most acceptable from all the Scriptures bearing on His coming. What matters most of all, friend, do you even believe He is coming back, whether you are pre-, post-, a-, or "pro-"? One preacher remarked that he was "promillennial." If there was going to be a millennium, he was all in favor of it! Jesus is coming back.

In 1 Thessalonians 5:3 it states: "While they are saying, 'Peace and safety!' then destruction will come upon them suddenly like birth pangs upon a woman with child; and they shall not escape."

He will come in a time when the leaders of nations, the heads of state, the dictators, the presidents, the kings are babbling, "We are not going to have war after all." The Russians, although still belligerent, are making "peace" over-tures. The Chinese Communists seemingly are softening up to the rest of the world. International relations will stay in a state of flux, but before Jesus comes, world leaders will be crying "peace." Then sudden destruction will fall, and there will be no escape.

Like it was in the days of Noah, God gave warning. Noah must have felt exhausted. He preached for 120 years! But no one would listen until the door of the ark was shut by God Himself, and the people began to scream and yell, "Let us in, Noah. We repent. We're sorry that we laughed at you, and that we wouldn't believe your message!" All of the world perished but eight souls.

God commanded, "There's no more time. Shut off the sermon, and I will shut the door."

What does all of this imply for the child of God? Mark it down. I repeat: no one on earth knows when Jesus is coming again.

But note in particular verses 2, 4, and 5. Verse 2 states that He is going to come "as a thief in the night." Verse 4 emphasizes: "But you, brethren, are not in darkness, that the day should overtake you like a thief."

You do not know, Christian, when He is coming, but you are not in darkness. In other words, you will not be sur-prised. You will be watching and waiting. You will be lifting up your eyes and longing for His coming. The One Who is coming is the Christian's friend. We will not view His com-ing as we would the intrusion of a robber or cat burglar. Verse 5 reminds us that we are the children of the day and the sons of light, not of darkness, which here symbolizes evil and wickedness.

The child of God has an avenue of escape—verses 9 and 10: "But since we are of the day, let us be sober, having put on the breastplate of faith and love, and as a helmet, the hope of salvation. For God has not destined us for wrath, but for obtaining salvation through our Lord Jesus Christ."

We are reserved, not for wrath, but for His tender mercies. We will be raptured with Him, to meet Him in the air. And when the worst is over on earth, we will come back to earth to reign and rule with Him. The Bible teaches that. It is not my private interpretation. However you arrange it, the Word of God declares that we will be "priests and kings" with Him!

Now gaze at the 10th verse: "Who died for us, that whether we are awake or asleep, we may live together with Him." That means, whether we are alive on earth when He comes for the saints or whether we have died in the body years before, we will be living together with Him. Those who have died in the Lord before will be resurrected, and then those "who are alive and remain unto the coming of the Lord" will be transformed and resurrected, and all of the believers will have a reunion with the Lord.

Then, after we have been with Him in heaven during the tribulation on earth, we will come back with Him. Look at what this Second Coming will mean to those who have forsaken the Lord. See 2 Thessalonians 1:7-9:

And to give relief to you who are afflicted and to us as well when the Lord Jesus shall be revealed from heaven with

His mighty angels in flaming fire, dealing out retribution to those who do not know God and to those who do not obey the gospel of our Lord Jesus. And those will pay the penalty of eternal destruction, away from the presence of the Lord and from the glory of His power.

If only we could impress this disturbing reality upon the lost. God, Who has given people every chance to receive Him, will return in flaming fire to deal out retribution. And they will pay the penalty of eternal destruction away from the presence of the Lord! If only we could press the urgency of reaching the lost upon lackadaisical Christians!

I am well aware that many teach there is no hell, that everyone is going to be saved, regardless of where they stood with God and how they responded to Him. If you believe the Bible, you just have to accept the fact of hell and punishment, and you have to reject so-called universalism which teaches that everyone is going to be saved, including Adolph Eichmann, Adolph Hitler, Ivan the Terrible, and every inhuman beast and rascal that has ever polluted the stream of human history.

How can one read passages like this and not believe in punishment and hell and retribution? The Bible has more to say about hell than heaven. Isn't it strange how many people believe in heaven but not hell? They are so happy and exude, "Oh, it's wonderful that there's a heaven." And they sing "How Beautiful Heaven Must Be." But they turn right around and shake their heads, "You'll never get me to believe that there's a hell."

But Jesus warned his hearers about the danger of "hell

fire." I would rather believe Him than a Bible-doubter. Hell is written across the pages of the Bible, but God does not want anyone go there. They choose to go there through their own volition. They reject God's gracious offer of forgiveness, eternal life, and heaven through the Lord Jesus.

What does the Second Coming mean for the saved? It promises that we will be with Him. Face to face with Christ our Savior! We shall know Him, and we shall see Him as He is.

> Beloved, now we are the children of God, and it has not appeared as yet what we shall be. We know that when He appears, we shall be like Him, because we shall see Him just as He is (1 John 3:2).

And the tables will turn. Second Thessalonians 1:6 makes it vivid: "For after all it is only just for God to repay with affliction those who afflict you [the believers]." All of the injustices of this earth will be rectified, will be righted, will be dealt with by a loving, but also just and righteous, God. The God of this universe will do right. I heard about the saintly old preacher who delivered a message at the funeral of man known to be lost, unless he repented while in a coma. The elderly preacher of the Word made his point, without hurting feelings or referring to the man as unsaved: "The Lord will do right." And He will. The scales will be balanced.

Through the years I have known people who all their lives, it seems, had been misunderstood. They had been unfairly treated, maligned, and hurt to the core, through no fault of their own. When the Lord returns, He will step in for those people who have unjustly suffered. Judgment is coming. Years ago there was an expression from Flip Wilson, "Here come de judge." Friend, it is no laughing matter. *The Judge is coming!*

> When He comes to be glorified with His saints on that day, and to be marveled at among all who have believed—for our testimony to you was believed (2 Thess. 1:10).

Amazing it is! Jesus shall be glorified in us. We are His workmanship, His building, His husbandry. We have been crafted in Him by the Holy Spirit.

What implication does that have for us? He is going to hold all of us up as a glorious example of what His grace has done. We who were sinners—lost, undone, hell-bound and hell-bent, low, weak, unworthy, incorrigible—are going to be pushed to the forefront as His trophies of redemption. Somehow the lost world is going to have a glimpse of the glory of God in us.

His return is going to be a time of rejoicing for the soul-winner. The last part of verse 10 goes: "For our testimony to you was believed." It is marvelous to witness and to testify on behalf of Christ, and then to have our witness believed. Why do so many Christians keep on plugging along, unsung and unpraised and unheralded? Because they are looking for the return of the Lord who will praise them, "Well done, thou good and faithful servant; thou hast been faithful over a few things, I will make thee ruler over many things: enter thou into the joy of thy Lord" (Matt. 25:21,23, KJV).

This is not a matter of vanity or pride but is the expectation of the Christian. If you win people here, I firmly believe you will encounter them in heaven. They will come up to you and exclaim, "Brother, sister, I was lost, and you shared Jesus with me. I am here in heaven because of your witness. If you hadn't come I might be in hell instead of here." Unknown preachers who served without fame or acclaim will have the redeemed running up to them with words like these, "Brother, you had a tough time in your church back there in the country. Your family did without. You were unjustly put down and criticized, but you led me to Jesus, and I never forgot. Bless you!" And it will make it all worthwhile. "When we all get to heaven, what a day of rejoicing that will be!"

In a brief word, what will happen between these two phases of His coming? In 2 Thessalonians 2, we are told what will happen on the earth. "For the mystery of lawlessness [iniquity, KJV] is already at work; only he who now restrains will do so until he is taken out of the way" (v. 7).

Here is a reference to the Holy Spirit, "the restraining One." He is here now holding back iniquity, lawlessness. Even with Him here, vile evil and gross wickedness abound. But can you imagine how much worse conditions would be if the Holy Spirit were not on earth today? For when God's children are taken up, I also believe the Holy Spirit will leave with them. All of the cesspools of people's minds will be unleashed across the earth. It will be a time of unprecedented perversity when the Holy Spirit departs.

More than that, "the man of sin," the antichrist, will be

revealed, and he will reign enshrouded by the very darkness of demonic hell.

> Let no one in any way deceive you, for it will not come unless the apostasy comes first, and the man of lawlessness is revealed, the son of destruction, who opposes and exalts himself above every so-called god or object of worship, so that he takes his seat in the temple of God, displaying himself as being God (2 Thess. 2:3-4).

The antichrist will be a real person, the representative of the devil, sitting on the throne in Jerusalem. He will be Satan-filled and Satan motivated.

The antichrist will be a dynamic leader who will "snow" the world. He will be a counterfeit of the Lord Himself. Remember that the devil tries to counterfeit everything concerning God. He will delude people into worshiping him and falling down at his feet. He will appear to have all the answers to the problems of the world. From all over the globe, people will attempt to make pilgrimages and worship him. For when the genuine church was caught away, people thought that was the last chance they would ever have for salvation (and they were correct). But this man of sin will offer them salvation, an imitation of God with no genuine salvation to proffer.

During that time no one will be able to buy or sell without the "mark of the beast" upon their foreheads, and unless they worship the antichrist, they will not be able to receive that mark.

What is to be our attitude while we wait for the rapture? Verses 13 and 17 answer the question.

But we should always give thanks to God for you, brethren beloved by the Lord, because God has chosen you from the beginning for salvation through sanctification by the Spirit and faith in the truth. . . . comfort and strengthen your hearts in every good work and word.

In this passage Paul also speaks about our calling "through our gospel, that you may gain glory of our Lord Jesus Christ" (v. 14). He asks the believers to "stand firm and hold to the traditions which were taught" (v. 15). Then he closes out the chapter with a benediction that God the Father and the Lord Jesus Christ "may comfort and strengthen your hearts in every good work and word" (vv. 16-17).

We are to rejoice that the Lord is coming. We are to stand fast, unwavering. "Steadfast, unmoveable, always abounding in the work of the Lord" (see 1 Cor. 15:58, KJV). Even though the world is flying into smithereens, we are to stand in the gap for God. Even when it seems the entire system is being sucked into the sewers of Satan! Sometimes people have warned me to "look out." That's not the admonition of the Scriptures. They counsel us to "look up." The Lord is coming. Look up! Rejoice! Stand fast! And comfort your hearts! "Wherefore comfort one another with these words," wrote Paul in 1 Thessalonians 4:18.

Because He is coming, and because there will be no second chances, we must urgently carry the message, as did John the Baptist, "Repent ye, for the kingdom of heaven is at hand." Your friends, your neighbors, your loved ones, your fellow workers are going to be left behind if the Lord comes soon.

Suppose you are sleeping in bed with your spouse and you are raptured, leaving your dear mate behind? And you are in a factory on an assembly line, and you are caught up, and your fellow workers are abandoned to the great tribulation? And you are riding to work in a carpool, and you are snatched away, but your fellow riders are left in misery? I want to ask you, Christian: How can you bear the thought? How can you live with it?

You are children of light, believers. Is it not time to let your light shine that others "may see your good works and glorify your Father which is in heaven"?

Who's in the dark? Those without the Light of the Lord Jesus Christ, the Light of the world. And His light is to shine through you.

Notes

Chapter 2—"Good News"

1. R. Earl Allen, *Jesus Loves Me* (Nashville: Broadman Press, 1979), p. 27.

2. A. C. Archibald, *This Is Our Gospel* (Nashville: Broadman Press, 1959), p. 71.

Chapter 3—"Don't Miss the Point"

1. Merrill D. Moore, *Found Faithful* (Nashville: Broadman Press, 1953), pp. 32-33.

2. Brian L. Harbour, *From Cover to Cover* (Nashville: Broadman Press, 1982), p. 240.

3. Copyright 1931 by E. Edwin Young. Printed in London, England, on same date.

Chapter 4—"No One Is an Island"

1. Clair M. Crissey, *Layman's Bible Book Commentary, Matthew* Vol. 15 (Nashville: Broadman Press, 1981), p. 47.

2. Words and tune WASHBURN, William J. Reynolds, 1971. © Copyright 1971 Broadman Press. All rights reserved.

Chapter 5—"What the Church Is"

1. Quoted in *A Treasury of Sermon Illustrations*, Edited by Charles L. Wallis (Nashville: Abingdon Press, 1950), p. 76.

2. Author Unknown.

163

Chapter 6—"Should We Be Here?"

1. Chester E. Swor, *The Best of Chester Swor* (Nashville: Broadman Press, 1981), pp. 159-160.

2. Author Unknown.

3. Paul W. Powell, *The Saint Peter Principle* (Nashville: Broadman Press, 1982), p.

4. Words and tune LEMMEL, Helen H. Lemmel, 1922. Copyright, 1922. Renewal 1950 by H. H. Lemmel. Assigned to Singspiration, Inc. All rights reserved. Used by permission.

Chapter 7—"Busy Here and There"

1. From Pearl Buck's *Fighting Angel*, quoted in *A Treausry of Sermon Illustrations*, p. 209.

2. E. P. Alldredge, *101 Expository Sermon Outlines* (Nashville: Broadman Press, 1941), p. 33.